Making Beautiful
Hemp & Bead Jewelry

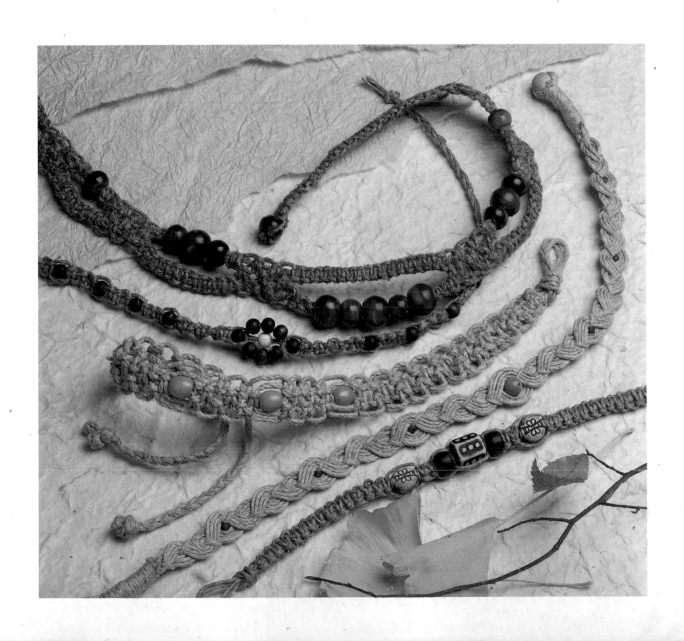

Making Beautiful

Hemp & Bead Jewelry

By Mickey Baskett

How to Hand-Tie Necklaces, Bracelets, Earrings, Keyrings,
Watches & Eyeglass Holders with Hemp

Sterling Publishing Co., Inc.

New York

Prolific Impressions Production Staff:

Editor: Mickey Baskett
Copy: Sylvia Carroll
Graphics: Dianne Miller, Prepress Xpress
Photography: Skye Mason, Jerry Mucklow
Proofing: Jim Baskett
Styling: Laney McClure

Acknowledgements

There were many talented artists that have contributed to designing the jewelry for this book. I wish to thank them for their willingness to share their talent and designs with other artists:

Miche Baskett
Marion Brizendine
Sylvia Carroll
Patty Cox
Sandy Dye
Kathryn Gould
Janet Zielke

Library of Congress Cataloging-in-Publication Data Available

10   9   8   7   6   5

81819

First paperback edition published in 1999 by
Sterling Publishing Company, Inc.
387 Park Avenue South, New York, N.Y. 10016
© 1998 by Prolific Impressions, Inc.
Distributed in Canada by Sterling Publishing
% Canadian Manda Group, One Atlantic Avenue, Suite 105
Toronto, Ontario, Canada M6K 3E7
Distributed in Great Britain by Chrysalis Books
64 Brewery Road, London N7 9NT, England
Distributed in Australia by Capricorn Link (Australia) Pty Ltd
P.O. Box 704, Windsor, NSW 2756 Australia
Printed in China
All rights reserved

Sterling ISBN 0-8069-6261-5 Trade
              0-8069-6275-5 Paper

Contents

Hooray For Hemp!

Hemp Cord Has Inspired a Revival of Macrame & Braided Jewelry

The current popularity of "all things hemp" has given new life to an old fiber art. Hemp cord—a natural fiber—can create beautiful and contemporary knotted jewelry designs to which this book attests. In these pages you will find 56 lovely jewelry projects which include chokers, necklaces, bracelets, anklets, earrings, watches, keyrings, and eyeglass holders.

In addition to the designs with instructions and diagrams, you will also find instructions for tying knots as well as macrame techniques and a discussion of supplies.

All the information you need is here. Add hemp to your accessory wardrobe, and don't forget your friends. Your birthday and holiday gift lists will be solved while you have fun being creative.

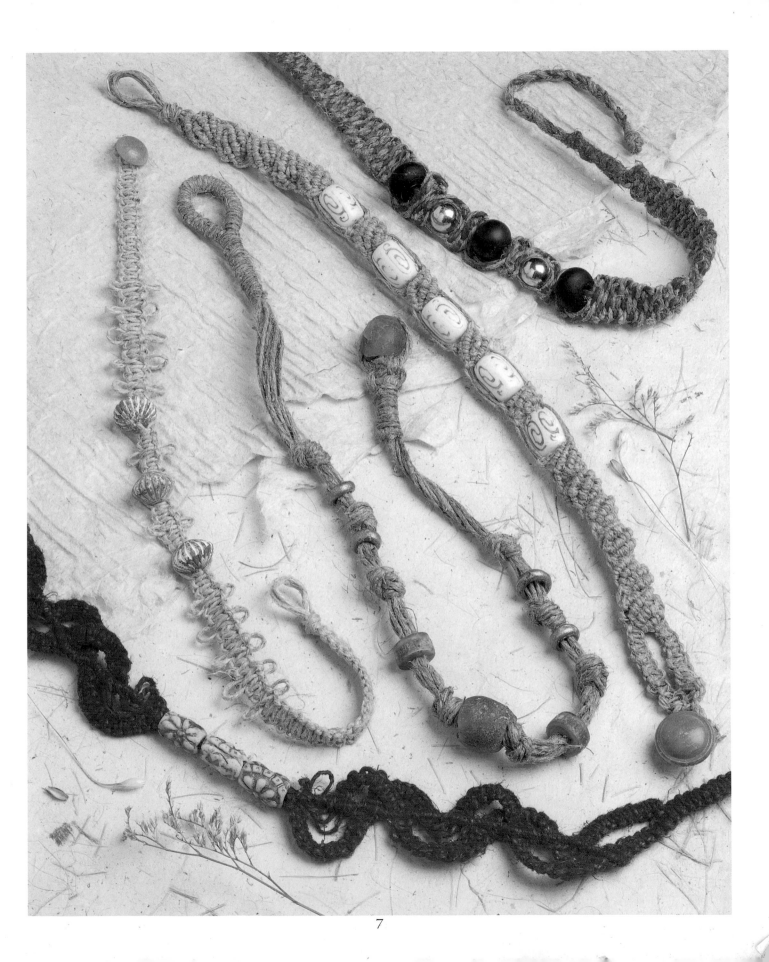

All About Hemp

Hemp is the hopeful answer to a myriad of needs in society, including the interests of people who otherwise seem to be at opposite poles in viewpoint. The environmentalist and the capitalist alike, for example, can find advantages and opportunities in this versatile commodity. This natural fiber answers many of the environmentalist's concerns, while it could considerably reduce our country's (or planet's) dependency on oil as a cheaper, safer fuel substitute. And for the fashion artist, it can be made into beautiful fabric and fiber art cord. These qualities, mentioned to demonstrate its universality, just scratch the surface of hemp's versatility and advantages.

Hemp Has A Long History

In the days of our forefathers, hemp was a common crop. A past publication of *The U.S. Department of Agriculture* has called hemp "the oldest cultivated fiber plant," mentioned how the crop improves the land, and said that it yields "one of the strongest and most durable fibers of commerce." In some areas of North America during Colonial times (Massachusetts, Connecticut, and Chesapeake, for instance), hemp production was so important that citizens were required by law to grow the plant. So much a part of America's history is connected with hemp that even the first two drafts of the U.S. constitution were written on hemp paper. The final draft is on animal skin.

Hemp Has A Variety of Uses

Paper is another wonder of hemp. It contains no dioxin or other toxic residues. A 1990 commentary for ABC News (by Hugh Downs) reports that: A single acre of hemp can produce the same amount of paper as four acres of trees. The trees take 20 years to harvest and hemp takes a single season. In warm climates, hemp can be harvested two even three times a year. It also grows in bad soil and restores the nutrients.

The "hurds" of hemp remaining after the fiber has been removed can be used to produce more than 25,000 products ranging from dynamite to cellophane to non-toxic paints and varnishes. Many of these products are now made with toxic petrochemicals. Since the growth of hemp was prohibited in the U.S. because it contains the drug known as marijuana (Mexican word for "hemp"), manufacturers have found other means of producing products. During World War II, the hemp crop was vital to the U.S. because the war had cut off access to fiber for textiles, rope, and other wartime needs. "Hemp For Victory" was a slogan for encouraging the growth of hemp. In 1943, over 100,000 acres of hemp was being grown in the U.S.

Hemp is really the environmentalist's dream. In the past, all oil lamps burned hemp seed oil until whale oil edged it out in the mid-nineteenth century. Later lamplights were fueled by petroleum and coal and, recently, radioactive energy. Hemp can be used to manufacture a variety of plastic products. It can provide a compostable styrofoam replacement. The seed oil can be converted into a valuable plastic resin. Some German manufacturers are developing snowboards and skateboards from hemp-based plastic. Plant-based plastics such as hemp and corn can be completely biodegradable.

Hemp—The Perfect Cord for Hand Tied Jewelry

Hemp fiber, including the cord used in this book, has great tensile strength and durability whether made into rope or fine lace. Hemp textiles with at least 50% hemp content block the sun's UV rays more effectively than other fabrics. Compared to cotton fibers, hemp fibers are longer, stronger, more lustrous and absorbent, and more mildew-resistant. Hemp fabrics also help keep the wearer cooler in summer and warmer in winter than do cottons or synthetics. Many innovations in the hemp textile industry are improving the qualities of hemp yarn, making it lighter weight and more uniform than before.

Hemp fibers, textiles, and items made of hemp are important for many countries around the world. There is a large movement afoot in the U.S. to reinstate the cultivation of fiber hemp as more and more people favor the environment-friendly and economically-sound products made from this plant. It's a wonderful way to enter the twenty-first century. ◇

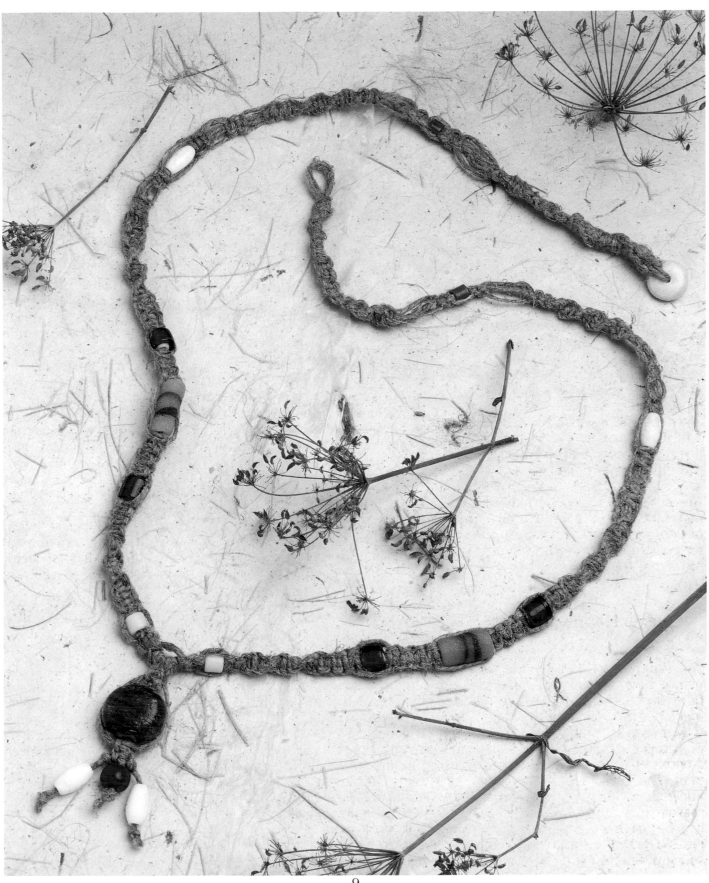

Supplies You Will Need

Hemp Cord

The jewelry in this book is made of 1mm pure hemp cord. It is available in a variety of colors as well as natural. Similar to linen, both spools and skeins of smaller amounts are available. Many craft stores carry this popular cord or can order it for you. There are also some shops specializing in clothing and other items made of hemp which carry hemp cord for macrame and other fiber arts.

Beads

A wide variety of colors, sizes and types of beads are used in these designs from earthy pottery and wood beads to sleek glass beads. Beads are available in craft shops and craft departments as well as your own box of old jewelry (or those at a flea market). The main requirement is that the holes are large enough to accommodate the number of cords that must be threaded through them. Remember, the thickness of each cord is 1mm in diameter. Pendants and hanging charms are also used on some necklaces. These have a hole or loop at the top for attaching them.

Because hemp has such a natural, earthy appeal, choose beads of natural materials to be consistent with this fashion look.

Knotting Board

Macrame knotting boards are made of a dense cardboard fiber approximately 3/4" thick. These have a pre-printed 1" grid that will help you keep your work even, and also help with measurements as you work. This type of board can be found at many craft shops, or shops specializing in jewelry and beading. The material of the macrame board is a type that T-pins stick into easily but hold firmly.

You can make your own macrame board with a ceiling tile available at building supply stores. If desired, you can also mark a 1" grid on the top surface with a permanent, non-smearing pen.

T-Pins

These are strong, sturdy T-shaped pins approximately 1-1/2" long with a cross bar at top for easy handling. There is much moving of the T-pins from place to place as you knot. Use the pins to hold your work firmly in place and to hold filler cords taut while tying knots around them.

Thick White Glue

This glue is often used to secure final knots before cutting away excess cordage. It is a flexible, clear-drying glue that will not show.

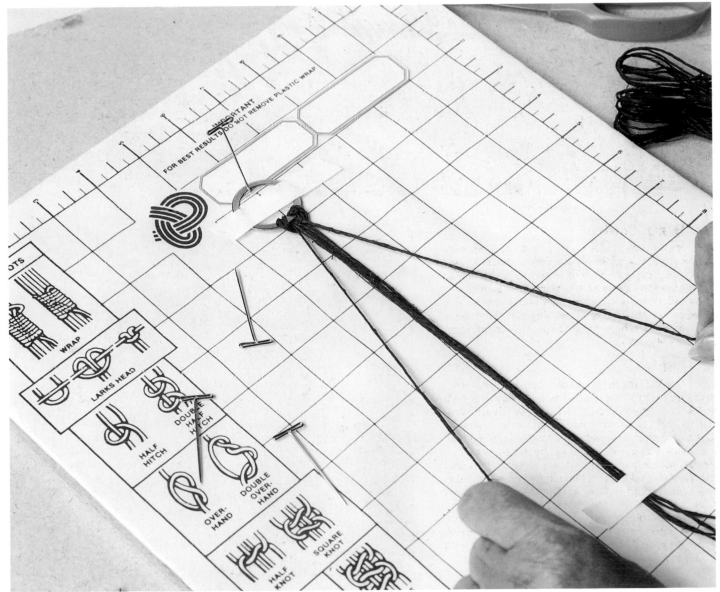

Macrame Terms & Techniques

Macrame Terms

Working Cords: All cords used in the design—both those tying the knots and those around which knots are tied. Often a cord is folded in half to produce two working cords.

Holding Cord: Cord around which Half Hitches, Double Half Hitches, or Lark's Heads are tied. The holding cord is held taut while tying the knots or mounting cords with Lark's Heads.

Knotting Cords: Cords with which the knots are tied. These are sometimes called "tying cords."

Filler Cords: Cords around which knots are tied. Filler cords are pulled taut and anchored with a T-pin while tying knots around them. A filler can also be something other than or in addition to cords. A frequent example in this book is where a knot is tied around the whole knotted end of a necklace as filler to create a loop or secure an end bead.

Round: When the ends of a row are joined with a knot to form a circle, it becomes a "round."

Sinnet: A strip of knots tied one under the other with the same working cords.

Picot: This refers to loops above a knot when extra cord is allowed in the knotting cords.

Row: A line of knots side by side tied with different working cords.

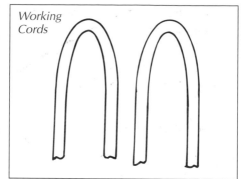

Working Cords

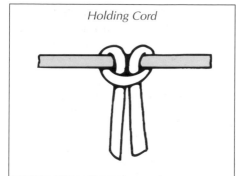

Holding Cord

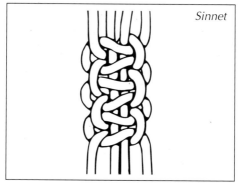

Knotting Cords

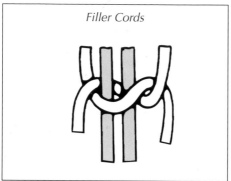

Filler Cords

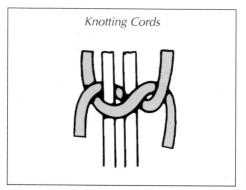

Sinnet

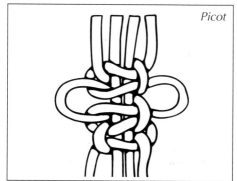

Picot

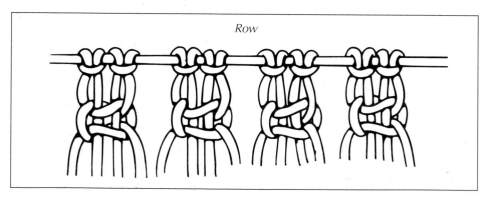

Row

Estimating Cord Lengths

When designing a project, you must estimate what length cords will be needed. There is no hard and fast rule for this since it depends on the design itself, knotting tension, and size of cord. Following are guidelines for cutting cord lengths which will produce two working cords (cords which are mounted with Lark's Heads or simply folded in half):

Open or Lacy Pattern: Cut cords 3 or 4 times the desired length of the finished project.
Medium Knotting Density: Cut cords 5 or 6 times desired finished length.
Dense or Solid Knotting: Cut cords 7 or 8 times desired finished length.

If cords are not going to produce two working cords, estimated lengths would be half as much as for those which are.

Also remember, when the same cords will be used as fillers throughout the design rather than tying any knots, these can be much shorter than your knotting cords.

How To Start a Necklace

This depends on the design. When the necklace is to be worked end to end, it can start by folding the cords, and this will also form the end loop for the closure. Skip the length of the loop and begin knotting.

When a necklace is worked from the center outward in both directions, it often begins with stringing the focal bead to the center of all cords which are aligned with each other. When there is a pendant, it is usually attached with a Lark's Heads. Cords are therefore first attached to the pendant, then worked from the center outward in both directions. Individual project instructions will address this issue.

Butterflying Cords

The cords can be very long when your project first begins. To avoid tangling and making cords generally easier to handle for tying knots, create a "butterfly bobbin" with each cord end as follows:

Referring to Fig. 1, wrap the cord around your thumb and pointer finger, wrapping it in a "figure 8" pattern. Wrap to within 10" of beginning knots. Loosely put a rubber band around the center of the "figure 8." As you need more cord, simply pull it from the bobbin. (It is not necessary to remove the rubber band to pull more cord free.)

Adding On a Cord With a Square Knot

This is done when the number of working cords need to be increased. Fold the new cord in half. Put it behind the cords on which it will be added. Use the two new cord ends as knotting cords and tie a Square Knot around the old cords as filler cords. Refer to Fig. 2.

Contrasting Color Filler Cords

An interesting color technique is to use filler cords of a color that contrasts with the knotting cords and leave spaces in the design for them to show through. In this book, the choker or double-bracelet project "Double Duty" is an example of this technique.

Stringing Beads

Generally beads are strung onto the filler cords while knotting cords are carried around the beads. Knotting resumes on the other side of the bead. If the hole will accommodate it, both filler and knotting cords are sometimes threaded through the bead. Again, knotting resumes on the other side of the bead.

To add a bead so that the hole is perpendicular to the necklace, thread cord(s) from one side through the bead in one direction and cord(s) from other side through the bead in the opposite direction. "Chain of Beads" and "Touches of Blue" projects show two versions of this.

Necklace Closures

The most often used closure for necklaces is the loop and bead closure.
Loop End: Loop cord ends back to end of necklace and tie a Square Knot or an Overhand Knot around end of necklace. Put thick white glue on knot and cut excess cordage. The looped area can be wrapped, wrapping with one of the cords around the other cords as shown in Fig. 3. Also one of the cords can be used to tie Continuous Half Hitches around area to be looped.

Another way to create a loop is to separate the cords into two groups, tie Alternating Half Hitches with each group for length of loop needed, then join groups again with one Overhand Knot. Put glue on knot and cut excess cordage.

Bead End: Thread all cords through a bead (or a shank button) and take them back to end of necklace. Tie a Square Knot or Overhand Knot around end of necklace. Put thick white glue on knot and cut excess cordage.

Two Overhand Knots tied with all working cords, one on top of the other, can substitute for a bead at end of necklace.

Instead of a bead, you can braid cord ends for several inches on side opposite loop. Secure braid with an Overhand Knot and trim cords. Tie the braid through the loop on other end of necklace.

Braids can, in fact, be used on both ends of necklace. To close, simply tie the braids together.

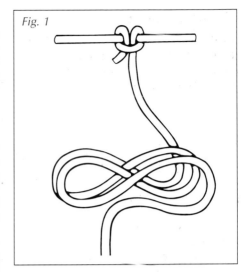

Fig. 1

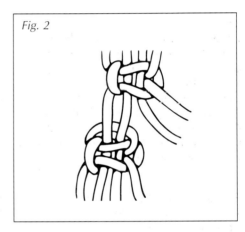

Fig. 2

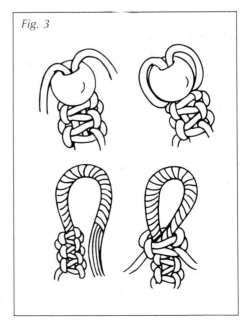

Fig. 3

Tying Macrame Knots

▪▪ The Overhand Knot

This knot is very common to most people and is used to start cords or to end them to prevent raveling. It is sometimes called a "simple knot." In this book it is often used with multiple cords tied together as one as well as with single cords to secure beads on cord ends.

▪▪ The Lark's Head Knot

The Lark's Head is used most often as the starting knot to mount cords onto a horizontal holding cord, ring, or other item. In this book it is also used to attach a tassel to a keyring project.

To make the Lark's Head, fold a cord in half and place the fold over the holding cord. Bring the loop down behind the holding cord and pull the two loose ends of cord through the loop. Pull tight.

▪▪ Lark's Head to Mount Cords on a Holding Cord

Often the Lark's Head is used to mount several cords on a holding cord to begin part of a pattern within the project.

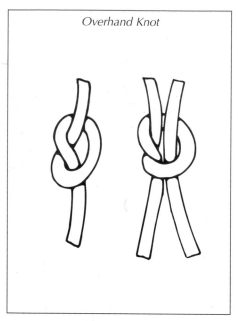

Overhand Knot

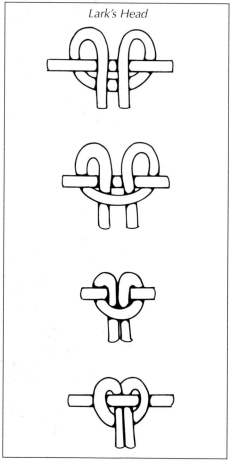

Lark's Head

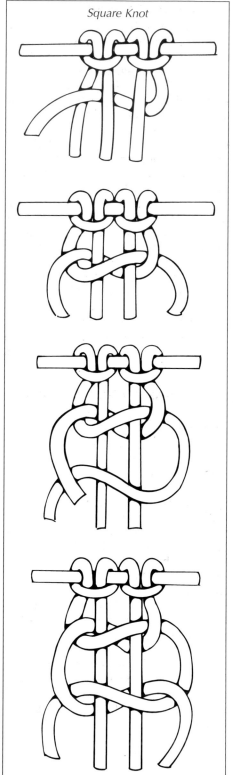

Square Knot

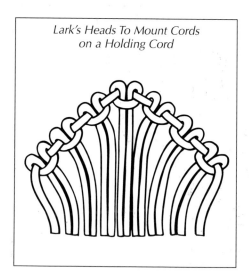

Lark's Heads To Mount Cords
on a Holding Cord

The Square Knot

The Square Knot is one of the basic macrame knots—probably the most important one. A wide variety of patterns can be achieved with this single knot.

The Square Knot is made in two steps. Follow the diagrams to take the knotting cords over the filler cords and through the loops for the first half, then for the second half. The second half reverses the over-and-under pattern executed by left and right knotting cords in the first half.

The two steps can be exchanged, if desired, to position the nubbin on the side of the knot you choose. In the order shown, the nubbin will be on the left side of the knot. If you tie the second half and then the first half, the nubbin will be on the right side of the knot.

Variations of Square Knots

The Square Knot can also be tied with more than two knotting cords and/or more than two filler cords.

Alternating Square Knots

To tie an Alternating Square Knot pattern, tie a row of Square Knots starting with the first four cords. For the second row, skip the first two cords and use the next four cords to tie a Square Knot. Continue row with each four cords successively. There will be two extra cords left at the end of the row. Each knot will use two cords each from the two knots above it, positioning the knot between those on the row above. For the next row, start with the first four cords. This will stagger these knots with the knots on the row above it. Again, each knot will use two cords from each of the two knots above it.

To tie an Alternating Square Knot pattern in a V-shape, tie decreasing rows of Alternating Square Knots by omitting one knot on each end of each row until you have a row with one center Square Knot.

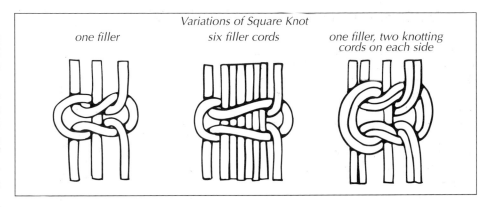

Variations of Square Knot

one filler *six filler cords* *one filler, two knotting cords on each side*

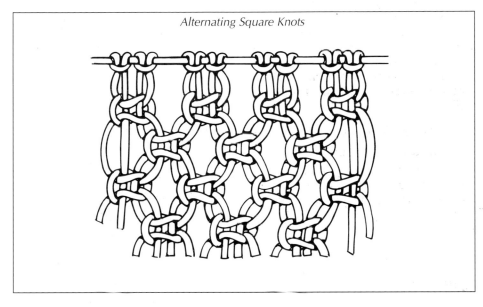

Alternating Square Knots

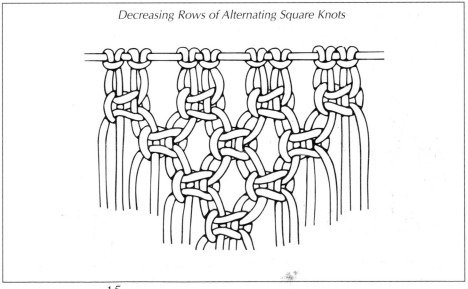

Decreasing Rows of Alternating Square Knots

Square Knots With Picots

Picots are loops that are formed by allowing extra cordage on knotting cords before tying the Square Knot. Two ways to create picots are:
(1) Place T-pins on each side, a short distance out from filler cords, and bring knotting cords around the T-pins before tying the knot; remove T-pins.
(2) Tie the knot lower on the filler cords than where you wish it to be, then push the knot up into position.

Square Knot Bobble

This is used as a decorative addition along a sinnet of Square Knots. Tie four Square Knots around the same filler cords. Bring the two filler cords up over the knots and down between the filler cords at the top of sinnet. Pull these cords down to form a bobble. Tie a Square Knot directly below the bobble to hold it firmly.

The Half Knot

The Half Knot is half a Square Knot, hence its name. Tie either the first or second half of the Square Knot to create this knot. When tied repeatedly around the same filler cords (a Half Knot sinnet) a twist occurs. These sinnets are often called "Half Knot Twists." When the first half of the Square Knot is used, the twist occurs in one direction; when the second half of the Square Knot is used, the twist occurs in the other direction. This is often important if, for instance, you wish to create a mirror image with Half Knot sinnets such as on the two sides of a necklace.

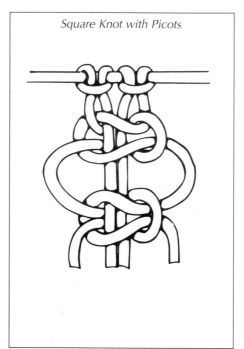

Square Knot with Picots

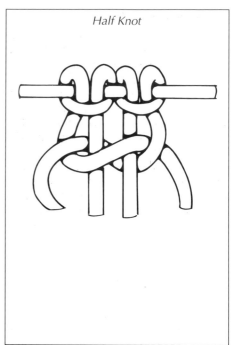

Half Knot

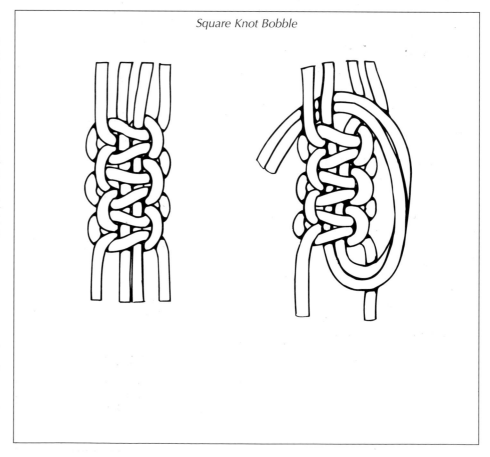

Square Knot Bobble

The Wrap Knot

The Wrap Knot (sometimes called a Gathering Knot) is used to bind many cords together for a neat appearance. This is frequently used at the ends of necklaces. To produce a Wrap Knot, form a loop with one end of a "wrap cord," placing loop up against filler cords and holding loop base securely. Begin at bottom and wrap the cords around all cords including the loop. Allow top of loop to be exposed. Place end of wrap cord through loop. Pull down on loop base end, pulling looped end inside the wrap so that it is in the center of the wrapping. Clip of cord ends.

The Half Hitch

The second most important knot in macrame is the Half Hitch. The simplest form is tied with two cords. The knotting cord makes a single loop around a filler or holding cord which is kept straight (horizontally, vertically, or diagonally).

Continuous Half Hitches (or Half Hitch Sinnet)

A continuing chain of Half Hitches along a holding cord is known as Continuous Half Hitches or a Half Hitch Sinnet. The sinnet will begin twisting.

Alternating Half Hitches (Chaining)

For this effect, worked with two cords (or two groups), the knotting cord/group and the holding cord/group change roles with every knot. First a Half Hitch is made around one cord as the holding cord. Then the previous knotting cord becomes the holding cord and vice versa for the next knot. These are alternated for the desired length of "chain" or Alternating Half Hitch sinnet.

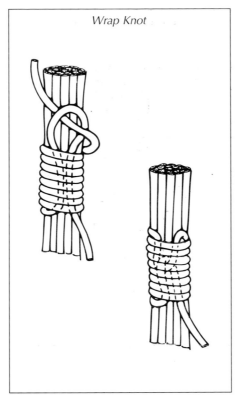

Wrap Knot

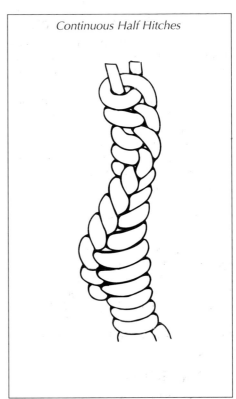

Continuous Half Hitches

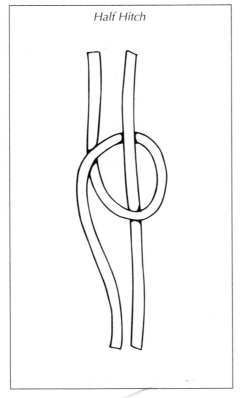

Half Hitch

Alternating Half Hitch Chain

▪▪ The Double Half Hitch (Clove Hitch)

This knot is really just two Half Hitches tied around a holding cord, but much more is done with it in macrame. Series of Double Half Hitches are used to create raised decorative lines and patterns that can go in most any direction. In this book, the Double Half Hitch rows run either diagonally or horizontally.

On the "Cat Toy" necklace watch project, a diamond pattern is created with diagonal Double Half Hitches. After tying the top of the diamond, all cords but the holding cords are woven diagonally across each other before tying the Double Half Hitch diagonal lines which create the bottom of the diamond.

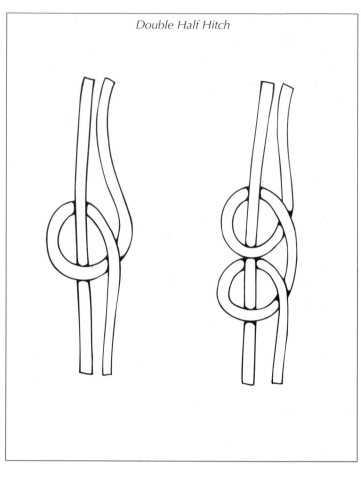

Double Half Hitch

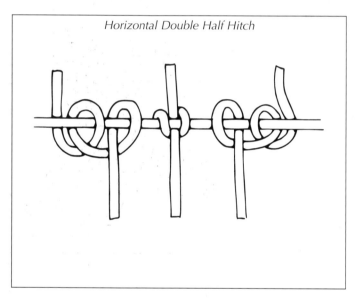

Horizontal Double Half Hitch

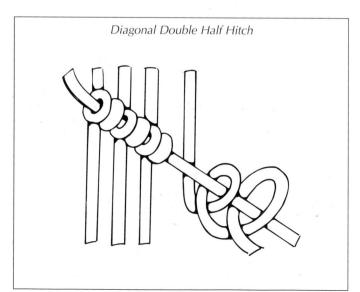

Diagonal Double Half Hitch

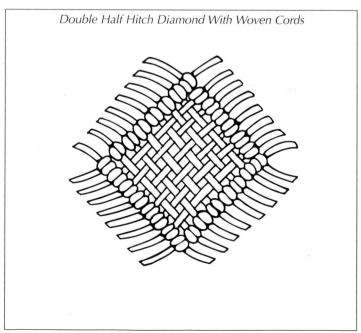

Double Half Hitch Diamond With Woven Cords

Chinese Crown Knot

The diagram shows a Chinese Crown knot tied with four cords. This knot must be tied with a number of cords that is divisible by four—four, eight, twelve. This knot is most easily tied with the cords placed upside down between your knees. Divide your cords into four equal groups. Follow the diagrams to complete this weaving process.

Berry Knot

To tie the Berry Knot, you must have 8 working cords. Tie a Square Knot with the left four cords and another with the right four cords. Use cord 5 as the holding cord and tie Double Half Hitches diagonally down to the left with cords 4 through 1. Tie three more rows of Double Half Hitches directly below the first, using cord 6, then 7, then 8 as holding cords for each row. Do not Double Half Hitch the holding cords of previous rows. Pull the holding cords tight and push up the diagonal rows of Double Half Hitches so the knot becomes slightly concave. Tie a tight Square Knot with cords 5-8 and another with cords 1-4. These will make the Berry Knot even more concave.

Josephine Knot

This knot is most attractive when tied with four, six, or eight cords. The diagrams show it with four cords. Make a loop with the two left cords. Lay the right cord over the loop, under the bottom and over the top of the first cords. Continue by bringing the right cords under the first cords, over themselves, and again under the first cords. To even the knots, pull the cords one at a time.

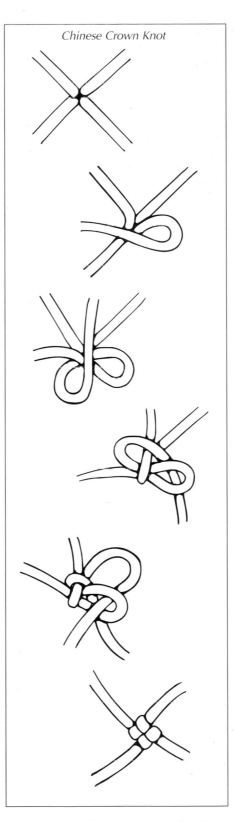

Chinese Crown Knot

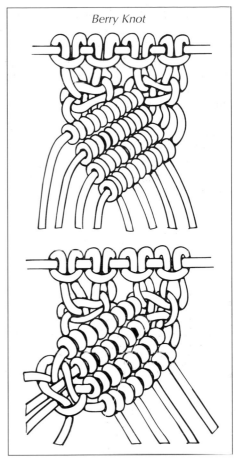

Berry Knot

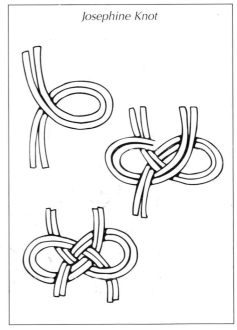

Josephine Knot

Braiding Techniques

Three-Part Flat Braid

The simplest of braids is the Three-Part Flat Braid, sometimes called the flat sinnet or pigtail braid. Divide the cords so that one cord is in your left hand and two cords are in your right hand. Braid by passing the uppermost cord of the larger group in front of the other cord in that same group and adding it to the back of the smaller group. Thus the smaller group becomes the larger. The process is then repeated over and over, taking the uppermost cord of the larger group and adding it to the back of the smaller group.

Four-Part Round Braid

Preliminary Step: Refer to Fig. 1. Bring cord 2 from the left across cord 3 and pass cord 1 under cord 3. Bring cord 4 over cord 2 and under cord 1. The two left cords have thus been brought to the right and the two right cords to the left.

Round Braiding: In the process of round braiding, the braiding cord is passed across the back, out on the opposite side, then brought across the front and returned to the side where it started. The first cord must be an outer left or right cord which crosses over, not under.

Refer to Fig. 2. Bring cord 3 (the outer left cord) across the back and push it out between the right cords (cords 2 and 1). Cross it over cord 1 and bring it back to the left next to cord 4.

Refer to Fig. 3. Pass cord 2 (the outer right cord) across the back (it will be a little loose) and push it out between the left cords (cords 4 and 3), then cross it over cord 3 so that it is back at the right next to cord 1.

Refer to Fig. 4. Pass the outer left cord (which is now cord 4) across the back and out between cords 1 and 2, cross it over cord 2 and back to the left. Pull work tight.

To continue: Pass the outer right cord across the back, bring it out between the two left cords, then cross it over the lower one and back to the right. Then pass the outer left cord across the back, bring it out between the two right cords, cross it over the lower one and out to the left. As you continue, cords 3 and 4 are always brought back to the left and cords 2 and 1 are always brought back to the right.

Six-Part Round Braid

Preliminary Step: Bring cord 3 over cord 4, under cord 5, and over cord 6. Then weave the other cords 2 and 1 over or under cords 4, 5, and 6 until you have cords 1, 2, and 3 at the right and cords 4, 5, and 6 at the left (Fig. 1)

Round Braiding: Refer to Fig. 2. Start with cord 3 (the upper right cord) which is an over-strand. Pass this cord across the back, bring it up between cords 4 and 5 at the left, then cross it over cord 5, pass it under cord 6 and back to the right.

Refer to Fig. 3. Pass cord 4 (the outer left strand) across the back, bring it up between cords 1 and 2, cross it over cord 1, pass it under cord 3 and back to the left.

Refer to Fig. 4. Continue by passing the upper cord, first the outer right and then the outer left, across the back, bringing it out on opposite side between the second and third cords from the bottom, then passing it over the second cord and under the bottom cord, and back to the side where it started. Pull your work up tight every time a cord has been brought back to the side where it started.

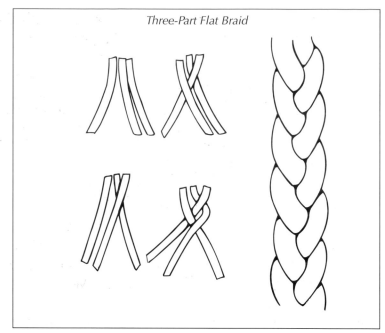

Three-Part Flat Braid

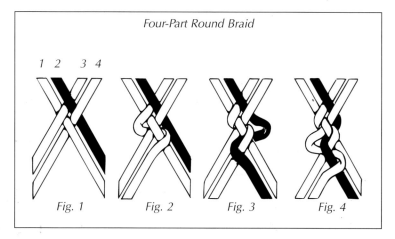

Four-Part Round Braid

1 2   3 4

Fig. 1   Fig. 2   Fig. 3   Fig. 4

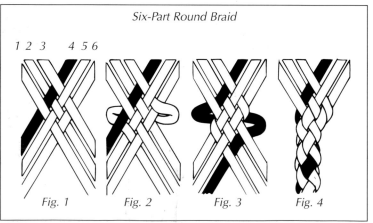

Six-Part Round Braid

1 2 3   4 5 6

Fig. 1   Fig. 2   Fig. 3   Fig. 4

Weaving Techniques

Weaving To Points On Right & Left Sides

(Shown With 6 Cords)

Weave with one cord at a time. As you weave from left to right, anchor all cords to the right of weaving cord with T-pins. Weave with cord 1 across all cords to the right. Anchor the weaving cord. Weave with cord 2 across cords to the right, including the previous weaving cord. Then anchor this weaving cord. Weave with cord 3 across cords to the right.

Reverse the process: Weave with what was the third weaving cord back to the left across all cords. Anchor the weaving cord on the left. Weave to the left with what was the second weaving cord; anchor weaving cord on left. Weave to the left with what was the first weaving cord.

Repeat the entire process for length desired.

Weaving With Cords Together Over Stationary Cords

(Shown With 3 Cords Woven Together)

Cords are used together as a triple strand. Weave all three together over, under, and over stationary cords to the right. Fold cords back around the outer (third) stationary cord, then weave over second cord, then under first cord. Fold cords up around outer (first) cord. Repeat the whole process for length desired.

Weaving With Cords Successively Over Stationary Cords

(Shown With 3 Cords Woven Successively)

Weave first cord on left across cords to its right. Weave with next cord on the left, including across the previous weaving cord. Weave with next cord on the left, including across the previous weaving cords.

Work the process in the other direction, weaving across cords to the left. Weave first with what was the first weaving cord, then with what was the second weaving cord, then with what was the third weaving cords. The weaving cords retain their order throughout—first weaving cord is used first whenever you change directions, second weaving cord is used second, and third weaving cord is used third.

Repeat the entire process for length desired.

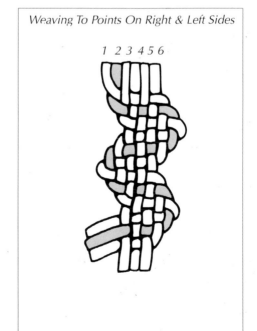

Weaving To Points On Right & Left Sides

1 2 3 4 5 6

Weavingwith Cords Together Over Stationary Cords

1 2 3 4 5 6

Weaving With Cords Successively Over Stationary Cords

1 2 3 4 5 6

Simplicity Choker

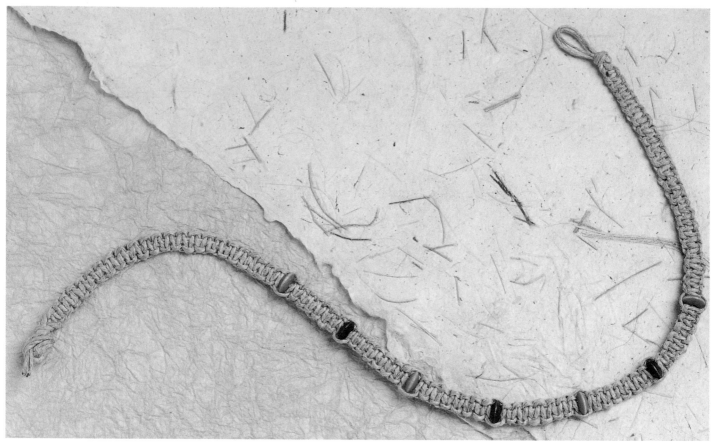

Finished length: 14-1/2" (end to end)
Change size by tying more or fewer knots at ends of choker.

MATERIALS
5-1/3 yds. 1mm natural-color hemp cord
Seven 8mm disk beads, 8mm wide—4 tan, 3 brown

KNOTS USED
Overhand Knot
Square Knot

CUTTING CORDS
Cut one 4-yd. cord.
Cut one 1-1/3-yd. cord.

INSTRUCTIONS
1. Find and align centers of the two cords and fold in half. At 1/2" from fold, tie an Overhand Knot with all cords together. This leaves a loop at end of choker and creates 4 working cords. Position shorter cords in center for filler cords, longer cords on outside for knotting cords. Follow Fig. 1 to begin knotting.
2. Tie a 3-1/2" sinnet of Square Knots.
3. Thread a tan bead on the filler cords.
4. Tie a 3/4" sinnet of Square Knots.
5. Thread a brown bead on the filler cords.
6. Repeat steps 4 and 5 until five more beads have been added, alternating colors.
7. End with a 3-1/2" sinnet of square knots.
8. Tie 3 Overhand Knots, one on top of the other. Trim excess cordage. �

Designed by Janet Zielke

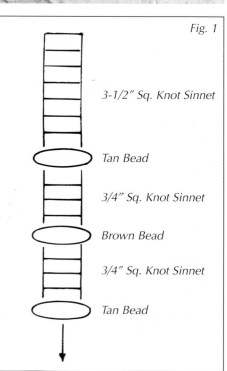

Fig. 1

3-1/2" Sq. Knot Sinnet

Tan Bead

3/4" Sq. Knot Sinnet

Brown Bead

3/4" Sq. Knot Sinnet

Tan Bead

Casual Chic Bracelet

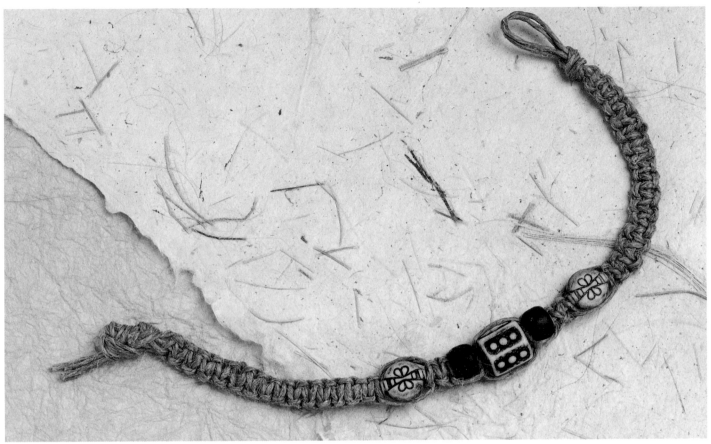

Finished length: 8" (end to end) + closure

MATERIALS
3 yds. 1mm natural-color hemp cord
Two matte black pony beads
Three denim-blue/white clay beads
    with designs –one 1/2" long planed
    cylinder, two 1/2" long flat ovals

KNOTS USED
Overhand Knot
Square Knot
Half Knot

CUTTING CORDS
Cut one 74" cord.
Cut one 26" cord.

INSTRUCTIONS
1. Find and align centers of the two cords
   and fold in half. At 1/2" from fold, tie
   an Overhand Knot all cords together.

This leaves a loop at end of choker and
creates 4 working cords. Position shorter cords in center for filler cords, longer
cords on outside for knotting cords.
Follow Fig. 1 while knotting.
2. Tie a 2-1/4" sinnet of Square Knots.
3. Thread a flat oval bead on the filler cords.
4. Tie 2 Square Knots.
5. Thread a black pony bead on filler
   cords.
6. Tie a Half Knot.
7. Thread cylinder bead on filler cords.
   This is center of necklace.
8. Repeat steps 6, 5, 4, 3, and 2 in that
   order.
9. Tie 2 Overhand Knots, one on top of
   the other. Trim excess cordage. ◇

Designed by Janet Zielke

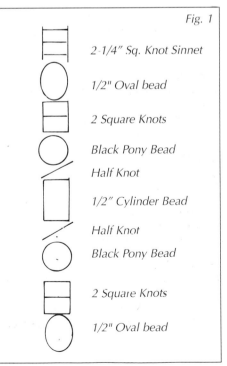

Fig. 1

2-1/4" Sq. Knot Sinnet

1/2" Oval bead

2 Square Knots

Black Pony Bead

Half Knot

1/2" Cylinder Bead

Half Knot

Black Pony Bead

2 Square Knots

1/2" Oval bead

Overhand Knot Necklaces

CHUNKY BEAUTY NECKLACE

Pictured bottom on page 25
Finished length: 19" (end to end)

MATERIALS

8 yds. of 1mm natural-color hemp cord
Two large-hole chunky green opaque glass beads, approx. 1/2" wide
Two large-hole unpolished amber short cylinder beads, approx. 1/4" long x 1/2" wide
Four brass spacers with large holes
Thick white glue

KNOTS USED

Overhand Knot
Wrap Knot

CUTTING CORDS

Cut eight 1-yd. cords.

INSTRUCTIONS

1. Follow Fig. 1. Align cords. String all 8 cords through a green bead, placing bead at center. Tie an Overhand Knot with all cords on each side close to bead.
2. Thread an amber bead on each side, positioning it 1" from Overhand Knot.

Skip 1" and tie an Overhand Knot on each side.
3. On each side: Skip 1", string a spacer to this position, tie an Overhand Knot close to spacer, and string another spacer up to Overhand Knot.
4. Skip 1" and tie an Overhand Knot on each side. Skip 4" of cord.
5. Bead end: Thread cords through remaining green bead. Bring cords back around bead and tie 2 Square Knots around cords to hold. Cut a 12" length from longest cord and use to tie a 1" Wrap Knot around cords. Clip excess cord lengths.
6. Loop end (Fig. 2): After skipping 4" of cord, use one long cord to wrap 3" of remaining cord. Fold wrapped section back into a loop that will go around end bead and continue wrapping around all cords for 1". Glue to hold. Clip excess cord lengths. ◇

Designed by Marion Brizendine

LONG & SHORT OF IT

Pictured top on page 25
Finished length: 14"-22" (circumference), with adjustable slide

MATERIALS

2-2/3 yds. to 3-1/3 yds. of 1mm natural color hemp cord
Multi-color clay bead, 5/8"
Two metal cone beads, 3/4" long
Four nugget beads, approx. 1/2" wide—2 amber, 2 green

KNOTS USED

Overhand Knot

CUTTING CORDS

Cut four cords each 24" long (for a longer necklace, cut cords 30" long)

INSTRUCTIONS

1. String clay bead to center of all 4 cords together.
2. Add a cone bead to each side of clay bead.
3. Add an amber bead to each side of each cone bead.
4. Add a green bead to each side of each amber bead.
5. Green beads have holes large enough for 4 more cords. Thread the 4 cords from opposite end of necklace through each in the opposite direction from first 4 cords.
6. Tie an Overhand Knot with all 4 cords at each end of necklace. To wear, loosen necklace to place over head. Pull on Overhand Knots to shorten. ◇

Designed by Marion Brizendine

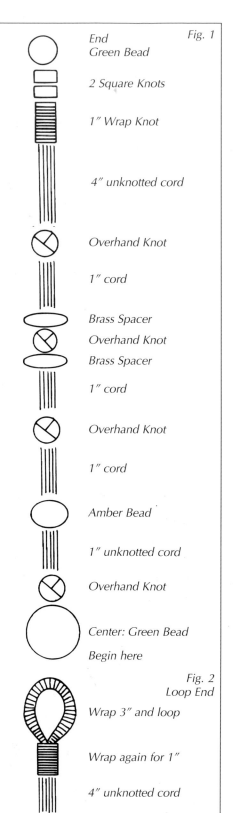

Fig. 1

End
Green Bead

2 Square Knots

1" Wrap Knot

4" unknotted cord

Overhand Knot

1" cord

Brass Spacer
Overhand Knot
Brass Spacer

1" cord

Overhand Knot

1" cord

Amber Bead

1" unknotted cord

Overhand Knot

Center: Green Bead

Begin here

Fig. 2
Loop End

Wrap 3" and loop

Wrap again for 1"

4" unknotted cord

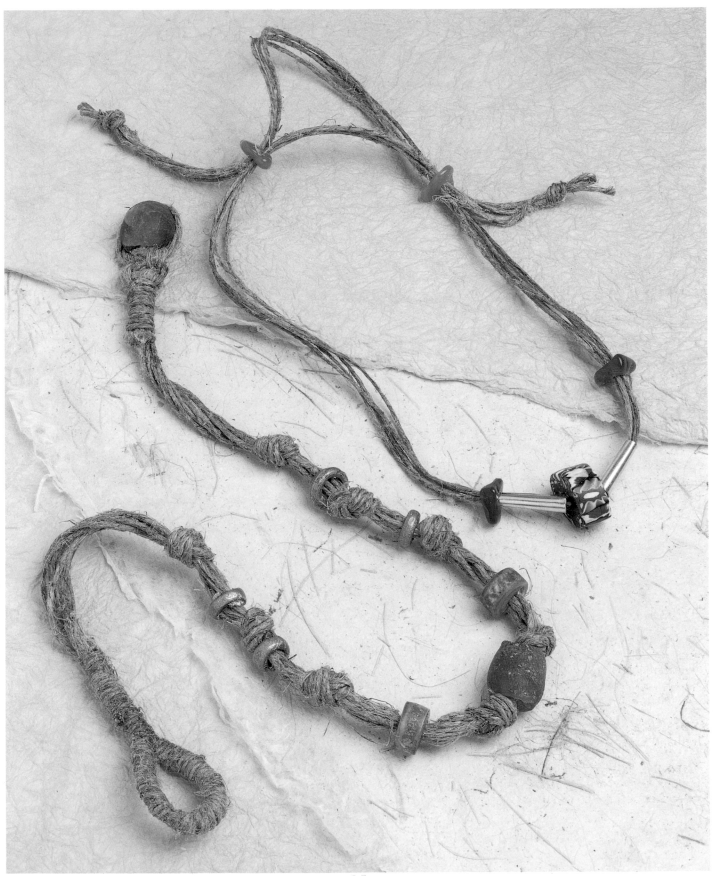

Spring Song Flower Ensemble

FLOWER BRACELET

Finished length: 9-1/2" (end to end) To lengthen or shorten increase or decrease lengths of braids on ends.

MATERIALS
2-2/3 yds. 1mm natural-color hemp cord
14 blue round wood beads, 1/4" or 6mm diam.
One white round wood bead, 1/4" or 6mm diam.

KNOTS USED
Overhand Knot
Three-Part Flat Braid
Square Knot
Half Knot

CUTTING CORDS
Cut two 1-yd. cords.
Cut one 24" cord.

INSTRUCTIONS
1. Align one end of all cords and tie an Overhand Knot close to end. Follow Fig. 1. Braid cords for 2", ending with short cord in center. Tie a Square Knot, using the short cord as a filler cord and 2 long cords as knotting cords.
2. String a blue bead on the filler cord.
3. Tie 3 Square Knots.
4. Repeat steps 2 and 3 twice.
5. Repeat step 2.
6. Tie one Half Knot. String 3 blue beads on each knotting cord. String white bead on filler cord. Bring cords back together (blue beads around white bead) and tie one Half Knot. This is center of bracelet.
7. Repeat steps 2 and 3 three times.
8. Repeat step 2 and tie a Square Knot.
9. Braid with a Three-Part Flat Braid for 2" and tie an Overhand Knot. Clip excess cordage. To wear, tie end braids together. ◇

FLOWER EARRINGS

Finished Length: 1-1/2" from wire

MATERIALS
1-1/3 yds. 1mm natural-color hemp cord
12 blue round wood beads, 1/8" or 4mm diam.
One white round wood bead, 1/4" or 6mm diam.
Pair of fish hook earwires

KNOTS USED
Half Knot
Square Knot
Overhand Knot

CUTTING CORDS
Cut four 12" cords.

INSTRUCTIONS
Repeat each step on second earring.
1. Center 2 cords on earwire. This creates 4 working cords.
2. Tie 7 Half Knots.
3. String 3 blue beads on each knotting cord. String white bead on the 2 filler cords.
4. Bring cords together under beads and tie 2 Square Knots.
5. Tie an Overhand Knot with all cords and trim cord ends. ◇

Necklace Instructions on page 28

Fig. 1

Overhand Knot

2" Three-Part Flat Braid

Square Knot
Blue bead

3 Square Knots

Blue bead

3 Square Knots

Blue bead

3 Square Knots

Blue bead
1 Half Knot

Blue bead

Center

White bead

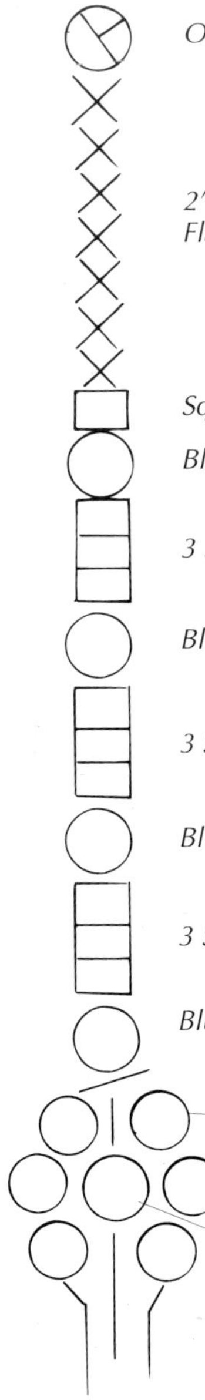

Repeat pattern in reverse.

Spring Song Flower Ensemble

FLOWER NECKLACE

Pictured on page 27
Finished length: 17" (end to end) To lengthen or shorten, increase or decrease lengths of braids on ends.

MATERIALS

6 yds. 1mm natural-color hemp cord
16 blue round wood beads, 1/4" or 6mm diam.
One white round wood bead, 1/4" or 6mm diam.

KNOTS USED

Overhand Knot
Three-Part Flat Braid
Square Knot
Half Knot

CUTTING CORDS

Cut two 2-1/2-yd. cords.
Cut one 30" cord.

INSTRUCTIONS

1. Align one end of all cords and tie an Overhand Knot close to end. Follow Fig. 1. Braid cords for 4-1/2", ending with short cord in center. Tie a Square Knot, using the short cord as a filler cord and 2 long cords as knotting cords.
2. String a blue bead on the filler cord.
3. Tie 3 Square Knots.
4. Repeat steps 2 and 3 twice more.
5. Repeat step 2.
6. Tie a 1-1/4" sinnet of Half Knots.
7. Repeat step 2.
8. Tie one Half Knot. String 3 blue beads on each knotting cord. String white bead on filler cord. Bring cords back together (blue beads around white bead) and tie one Half Knot. This is center of necklace.
9. Repeat step 2.
10. Repeat step 6.
11. Repeat steps 2 and 3 three times.
12. Repeat step 2 and tie a Square Knot.
13. Braid with a Three-Part Flat Braid for 4-1/2" and tie an Overhand Knot. Clip excess cordage. To wear, tie end braids together. ◇

Designed by Janet Zielke

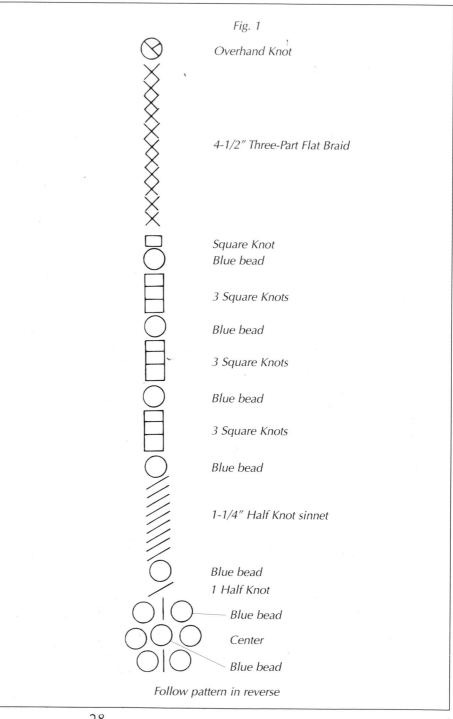

Fig. 1

Overhand Knot

4-1/2" Three-Part Flat Braid

Square Knot
Blue bead

3 Square Knots

Blue bead

3 Square Knots

Blue bead

3 Square Knots

Blue bead

1-1/4" Half Knot sinnet

Blue bead
1 Half Knot

Blue bead

Center

Blue bead

Follow pattern in reverse

Three Easy Chokers

DAYS OF AUGUST

Pictured center on page 31
Finished length: 15" (end to end)

MATERIALS
5 yds. 1mm orange hemp cord
White/orange oval flower design bead,
   5/8" long
Round wood bead, approx. 1/2" diam.
Thick white glue

KNOTS USED
Half Knot
Square Knot

CUTTING CORDS
Cut two 1-1/2-yd. cords (knotting cords)
Cut two 36" cords (filler cords)

INSTRUCTIONS
1. Follow Fig. 1. Find and align centers of all 4 cords. String flower bead to center. Work in both directions from center to ends of necklace, repeating each step on each side up to closure steps. Use long cords for knotting cords, short cords for filler cords.
2. Tie 1-1/2" of Half Knots.
3. Tie 3/4" of Square Knots.
4. Tie 1/2" of Half Knots.
5. Tie 1" of Square Knots.
6. Repeat steps 4 and 5, then step 4.
7. Tie 1-1/2" of Square Knots.
8. Loop end: Use the longest cord to wrap the other 3 cords for 1-1/2". Fold wrapped area back over end of necklace to form a loop. Tie a Square Knot around end of necklace. Put glue on knot. When dry, clip excess cordage.
9. Bead end (Fig. 2): Thread cords through wood bead. Cut filler cords off even with bead. Bring knotting cords back around bead and tie a Square Knot with them around end of necklace. Put glue on knot. When dry, clip excess cordage. ◊

Designed by Kathryn Gould

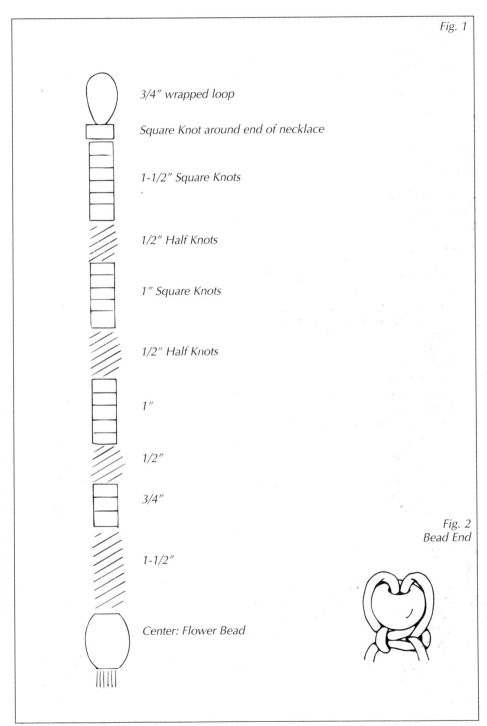

Fig. 1

3/4" wrapped loop

Square Knot around end of necklace

1-1/2" Square Knots

1/2" Half Knots

1" Square Knots

1/2" Half Knots

1"

1/2"

3/4"

1-1/2"

Center: Flower Bead

Fig. 2
Bead End

Three Easy Chokers

TURQUOISE CHARM

Pictured bottom on page 31
Finished length: 15-1/2" (end to end)

MATERIALS
4-1/3 yds. 1mm turquoise hemp cord
Three round turquoise beads, 1/2" diam.
One round blue wood bead, 3/8" diam.
Thick white glue

KNOTS USED
Square Knot

CUTTING CORDS
Cut two 1-1/3-yd. cords (knotting cords)
Cut two 30" cords (filler cords)

INSTRUCTIONS
1. Follow Fig. 1. Find and align centers of all 4 cords. String all 3 turquoise beads to center. Work in both directions from center to ends of necklace, repeating each step on each side up to closure steps. Use long cords for knotting cords, short cords for filler cords.

2. Tie 3 Square Knots
3. Skip 1/4" space.
4. Repeat steps 2 and 3 to ends of necklace (approximately 10 times), then repeat step 2.
5. Loop end: Use the longest cord to wrap the other 3 cords for 1-1/2". Fold wrapped area back over end of necklace to form a loop. Tie a Square Knot around end of necklace. Put glue on knot. When dry, clip excess cordage.
6. Bead end (Refer to Fig. 2 on page 29): Thread cords through wood bead. Cut filler cords off even with bead. Bring knotting cords back around bead and tie a Square Knot with them around end of necklace. Put glue on knot. When dry, clip excess cordage. ◌

Designed by Kathryn Gould

DOUBLE DUTY

Pictured top on page 31
Finished length: 15" (end to end)

MATERIALS
4-2/3 yds. of 1mm dk. blue hemp cord
1-1/3 yds. of 1mm natural-color hemp cord
Dk. blue wood bead, 3/8" diam.
Thick white glue

KNOTS USED
Overhand Knot
Square Knot

INSTRUCTIONS
1. Fold blue cord in half. At 1/2" from fold, tie an Overhand Knot with the 2 blue working cords together. This forms an end loop.
2. Fold natural cord in half and pin fold at Overhand Knot between the 2 blue working cords. There are now 4 working cords—2 blue and 2 natural. Use the blue cords as knotting cords and the natural cords as fillers.
3. Tie 4 Square Knots. Skip approximately 1/4" so that natural color filler cords show. Repeat to end of necklace (approximately 16 more times). Tie 4 more Square Knots.
4. Bead end (Refer to Fig. 2 on page 29): Thread cords through wood bead. Cut filler cords off even with bead. Bring knotting cords back around bead and tie a Square Knot with them around end of necklace. Put glue on knot. When dry, clip excess cordage. ◌

Designed by Kathryn Gould

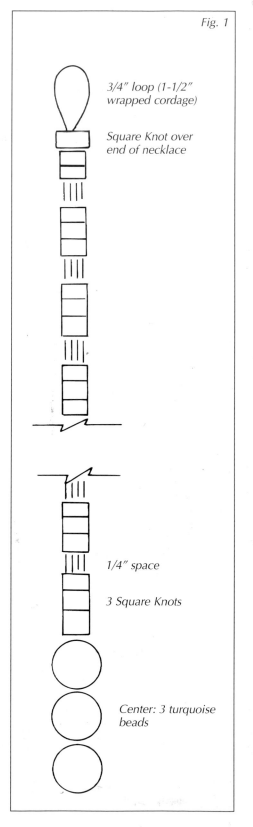

Fig. 1

3/4" loop (1-1/2" wrapped cordage)

Square Knot over end of necklace

1/4" space

3 Square Knots

Center: 3 turquoise beads

Natural and Blue

COME TO THE DANCE BRACELET

Pictured left on page 33
Finished length: 8" (end to end) + ties

MATERIALS
6-3/4 yds. 1mm natural-color hemp
Medium blue oval bead, 1/2"
Four medium blue round beads, 1/4" diam.
Four black round beads, 3/16" diam.

KNOTS USED
Square Knot
Overhand Knot
Three-Part Flat Braid

CUTTING CORDS
Cut three 2-1/4-yd. cords

INSTRUCTIONS
1. Align centers of all 6 cords. Braid 2" of Three-Part Flat Braid in center of cords. Bring ends of braid together to form a loop. There will now be 6 working cords.
2. Tie 4 Square Knots, using 4 knotting cords and 2 filler cords.
3. Tie 2 Square Knots with the center 4 cords.
4. Tie 2 Square Knots with the left 3 cords (one filler cord) and 2 Square Knots with the right 3 cords (side by side sinnets).
5. Repeat steps 3 and 4 three more times.
6. Thread a black bead on each outer cord (cords 1 and 6).
7. Repeat steps 3 and 4.
8. Repeat step 6 with medium blue round beads.
9. Repeat steps 3 and 4.
10. Tie 1 Square Knot with center 4 cords.
11. Thread oval bead on the 2 filler cords.
12. Follow Fig. 1 and above instructions in reverse for other half of necklace, ending with the 3- cord side by side sinnets.
13. Tie a Square Knot with all cords (4 knotting cords and 2 filler cords).
14. Divide cords into two 3-cord groups and braid each for 3" with a Three-Part Flat Braid. Tie an Overhand Knot with each group. Tie these braids through loop at other end of necklace to fasten necklace. ◇

Designed by Miche Baskett

TWIST OF NATURE CHOKER

Pictured right on page 33
Finished length: 16" (end to end) + ties

MATERIALS
11 yds. of 1mm natural-color hemp cord
One multi-color bead, 1" long
Four blue spaghetti beads, 1" long

KNOTS USED
Half Knot
Overhand Knot

CUTTING CORDS
Cut two 5-yd. cords (knotting cords)
Cut one 1-yd. cord (filler cord)

INSTRUCTIONS
1. Align ends of all 3 cords. Drop down 3" and tie an Overhand Knot with all cords. Place the long cords on outside and short cord in center.
2. Tie 6" of Half Knots.
3. Thread a spaghetti bead on each knotting cord.
4. Tie 2" of Half Knots.
5. Place oval bead on filler cord.
6. Follow above instructions in reverse (through step 2) for other half of necklace.
7. Tie an Overhand Knot with all cords.
8. Make a loop with filler cord and tie an Overhand Knot with it around previous Overhand Knot. Clip excess on all three cords. ◇

Designed by Miche Baskett

Additional project instructons on page 34

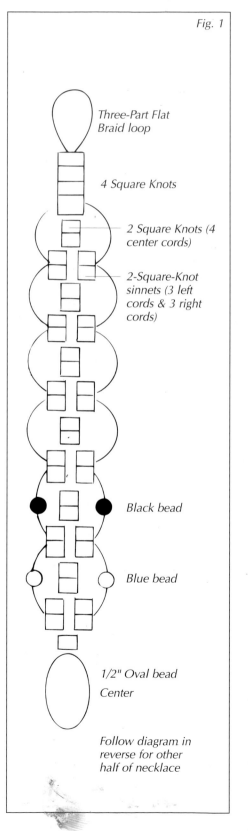

Fig. 1

Three-Part Flat Braid loop

4 Square Knots

2 Square Knots (4 center cords)

2-Square-Knot sinnets (3 left cords & 3 right cords)

Black bead

Blue bead

1/2" Oval bead

Center

Follow diagram in reverse for other half of necklace

Natural and Blue

Beautiful Symmetry Necklace

Pictured center on page 33

Finished length: 14" (end to end). To lengthen, repeat steps 3 and 4 up to three more times on each side of necklace.

Materials
20 yds. 1mm natural-color hemp cord
Blue ceramic flowered tube bead, 1-1/8" long
Four blue wood cube beads, 1/4" or 6mm wide

Knots Used
Overhand Knot
Square Knot
Alternating Square Knots

Cutting Cords
Cut eight 2-1/2-yd. cords.

Instructions
1. Align cords and tie one Overhand Knot with all cords. Follow Fig. 1 as you work.
2. Skip 3/4" and tie a Square Knot with all cords, using 4 knotting cords and 4 filler cords.
3. Tie a Square Knot with the left 4 cords and a Square Knot with the right 4 cords.
4. Tie a Square Knot with the center 4 cords.
5. Repeat steps 3 and 4 eight times.
6. Repeat step 3.
7. Thread a square wood bead on center 2 cords. Tie a Square Knot under bead with the center 4 cords.
8. Repeat steps 3 and 4, then step 3.
9. Repeat step 7, then step 3.
10. Thread large bead onto center 4 cords. This is the center of necklace.
11. Repeat pattern in reverse through step 3.
12. Tie a Square Knot with all cords, using 4 knotting cords and 4 filler cords.
13. Tie 2 Overhand Knots with all cords. Trim cords. ◇

Designed by Janet Zielke

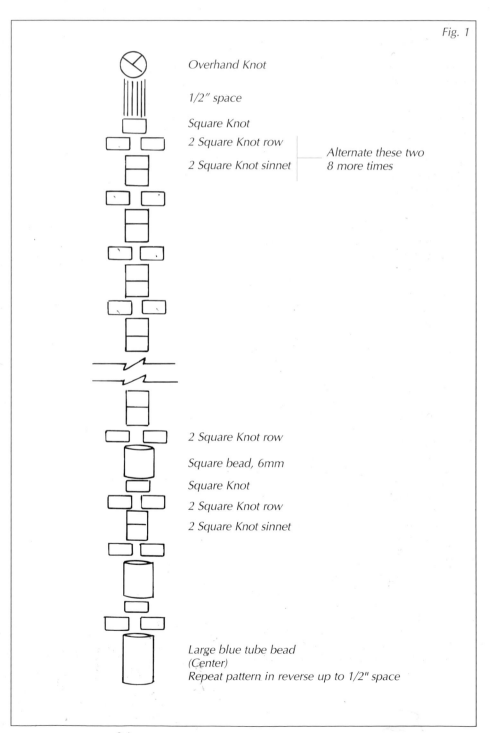

Fig. 1

Overhand Knot

1/2" space

Square Knot

2 Square Knot row

2 Square Knot sinnet

Alternate these two
8 more times

2 Square Knot row

Square bead, 6mm

Square Knot

2 Square Knot row

2 Square Knot sinnet

Large blue tube bead
(Center)
Repeat pattern in reverse up to 1/2" space

Ocean Waves Choker

Finished length: 15-1/2" (end to end)

MATERIALS

13.5

4-1/2 yds. of 1mm natural-color hemp cord
One round wood bead, 3/8" diam.
Six blue beads, 1/8"
One green bead, 5/16"

KNOTS USED

Wrap Knot
Three-Part Flat Braid

CUTTING CORDS

Cut four 3-yd. cords
Cut one 1-1/2-yd. cords

INSTRUCTIONS

1. Align the 4 long cords and thread wood bead to center. Bring all cords together under the bead. Use one end of the 1-1/2-yd. cord to tie a Wrap Knot around all cords so that the long end of the wrap cord extends downward with the other working cords. There are now 9 working cords.
2. Divide the cords from the bead into two groups of 4 cords each. The Wrapping Cord will comprise a third braid "group" of only one cord.
3. Tie a Three-Part Flat Braid for approximately 1-1/2" with these three groups. Keep the cords in the 4-cord groups side by side to create flat groups.
4. When single-cord crosses to the front from the left side, string a blue bead on it before continuing braid. Position bead in center of braid.
5. Continue braid. Next time, let the single cord cross from the left without a bead. But the next time it crosses from the left, add another blue bead as in step 4.
6. Repeat step 5.
7. Repeat step 5 but when it is time to add a bead, add the larger green bead.
8. Follow above instructions in reverse through step 3 for other half of necklace.
9. With one cord, wrap other cords for 3". Turn wrapped portion back onto end of necklace to form a loop. Wrap around all cords back toward center of necklace for 1" with a Wrap Knot. ◇

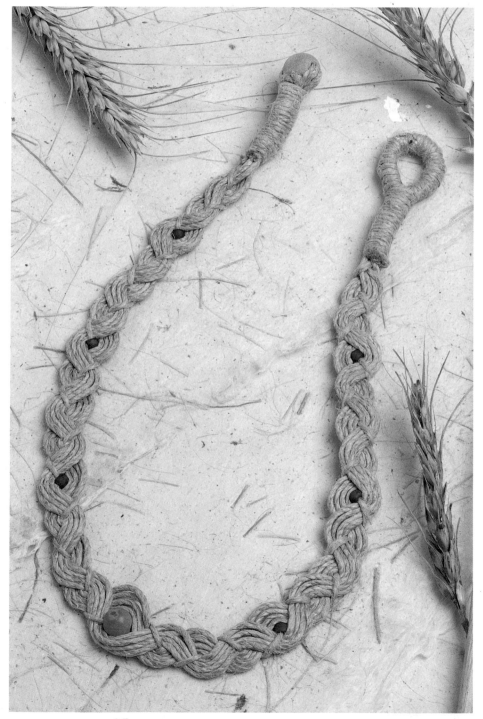

Beaded Bracelets and Anklets

MORNING-GLORY MAGIC BRACELET

Pictured left on page 37
*Finished length: 6-1/2" (end to end). For a 7-1/2" length,
add 5 more Half Knots to each end.*

MATERIALS
2-2/3 yds. 1mm dk. natural hemp cord
Purple Millefiori morning-glory bead,
    1/2" wide
Two transparent purple pony beads

KNOTS USED
Overhand Knot
Half Knot
Square Knot

CUTTING CORDS
Cut one 2-yd. cord.
Cut one 24" cord.

INSTRUCTIONS
1. Align centers of cords and fold in half. At 1/2" from fold, tie an Overhand Knot with all cords. This creates a loop on one end and 4 working cords. Use longer cords as knotting cords and shorter cords as filler cords. Follow Fig. 1 as you work.
2. Tie a 1-3/4" sinnet of Half Knots.
3. Tie 3 Square Knots.
4. String a pony bead onto filler cords.
5. Tie 3 Square Knots.
6. String the morning-glory bead onto filler cords. This is center of necklace.
7. Repeat steps 5, 4, 3, and 2 in that order.
8. Tie an Overhand Knot with all cords. Trim cords. ◇

Designed by Janet Zielke

BELLS ON HER WRIST

Pictured second from left on page 37
Finished length: 8-1/2" (end to end)

MATERIALS
3-1/2 yds. of 1mm natural color hemp
20 goldtone bells, 1/4" diam.
Goldtone shank button, 1/2" diam.
Optional: Thick white glue

KNOTS USED
Overhand Knot
Half Knot
Square Knot (no fillers)

CUTTING CORDS
Cut one 2-1/2-yd. cord
Cut one 1-yd. cord

INSTRUCTIONS
1. Align centers of cords. Tie all cords together with an Overhand Knot, leaving a 1/2" loop. There are 4 working cords. Follow Fig. 2 as you work.
2. Tie 2 Half Knots. Add a bell to the right knotting cord. Repeat until bracelet is desired length.
3. Tie a goldtone shank button on center cords. Tie all cords together with a Square Knot (use 4 knotting cords, no fillers). Optional: Apply a dot of thick white glue to ending knot. Clip ends. ◇

Designed by Patti Cox

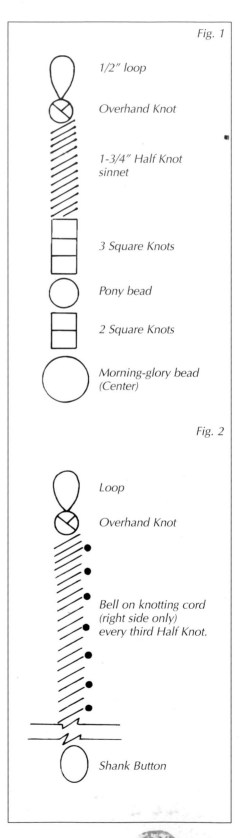

Fig. 1

1/2" loop

Overhand Knot

1-3/4" Half Knot sinnet

3 Square Knots

Pony bead

2 Square Knots

Morning-glory bead (Center)

Fig. 2

Loop

Overhand Knot

Bell on knotting cord (right side only) every third Half Knot.

Shank Button

Beaded Bracelets and Anklets

TOUCH OF NATURE ANKLET

Pictured bottom on page 37
Finished length: 11" (end to end)

MATERIALS
3-3/4 yds. 1mm natural color hemp cord
Six wood cube beads, 1/4"—2 yellow
  and 4 brown
Thick white glue

KNOTS USED
Overhand Knot
Six-Part Round Braid

CUTTING CORDS
Cut three 45" cords

INSTRUCTIONS
1. Fold the 3 cords in half. At 3/4"
   from fold, tie an Overhand Knot
   with all cords, forming a 3/4" loop.
   There are 6 working cords.
2. Braid for 2-1/2" with a Six-Part
   Round Braid.
3. Place a bead on one cord.
4. Braid for 1/2" and place a bead on
   one cord.
5. Braid for 1" and place a bead on
   one cord.
6. Repeat steps 4 and 5.
7. Repeat step 4.
8. Repeat step 2.
9. Tie 2 Overhand Knots on top of
   each other to form a "bead" to go
   through loop at other end.
10. Put glue on knot. When dry, clip
    cords close to knot.

Designed by Miche Baskett

Fig. 1

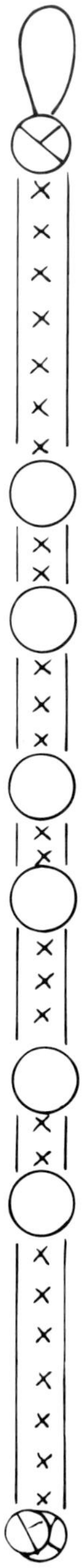

3/4" loop

Overhand Knot

2-1/2" of Six-Part
Round Braid

Brown Bead
1/2" Braid
Yellow Bead
1" Braid

Brown Bead
1/2" Braid
Brown Bead
1" Braid

Yellow Bead
1/2" Braid
Brown Bead

2-1/2" Braid

2 Overhand Knots

BAND OF FLOWERS BRACELET

Pictured right on page 37
Finished length: 7-1/2" (end to end)

MATERIALS
6 yds. 1mm natural-color hemp cord
6 round navy blue wood beads, 3/8" diam.
36 round rust wood beads, 1/8" diam.
Wood spacer type bead, 1/2" wide
Thick white glue

KNOTS USED
Lark's Head
Overhand Knot
Square Knot
Continuous Half Hitches

CUTTING CORDS
Cut two 3-yd. cords.

INSTRUCTIONS
1. Follow Fig. 1. Fold the 2 cords in half and attach to the spacer type bead with a Lark's Head.
2. Tie an Overhand Knot with the 4 working cords close to the bead.
3. Tie 4 Square Knots.
4. String 3 rust beads on each knotting cord (6 beads total). String one navy bead onto the 2 filler cords together.
5. Repeat steps 3 and 4 five more times, then step 3.
6. Loop end: Using longest cord as knotting cord, tie Continuous Half Hitches around other cords for 2-1/2". Bend this sinnet into a loop back to end of bracelet. Tie a Square Knot around end of bracelet. Add glue to knot. When dry, clip excess cordage. ◇

By Marion Brizendine

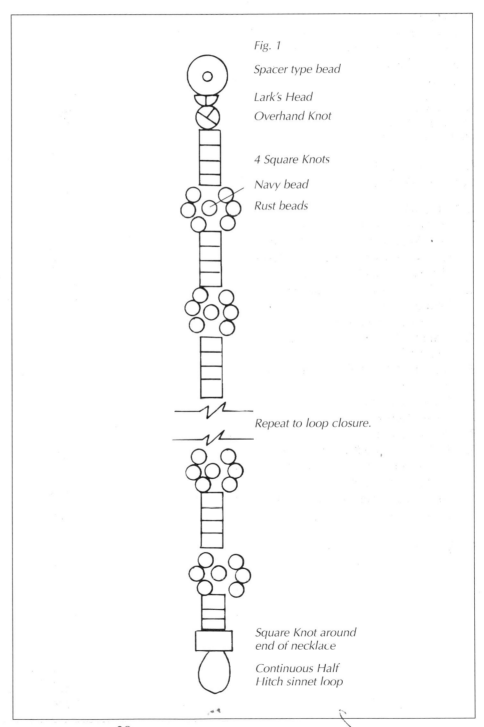

Fig. 1

Spacer type bead

Lark's Head
Overhand Knot

4 Square Knots

Navy bead
Rust beads

Repeat to loop closure.

Square Knot around end of necklace

Continuous Half Hitch sinnet loop

Berry Beautiful Choker

Finished length: 16" (end to end)

MATERIALS
36 yds. 1mm dk. blue hemp
1-1/4" oval goldtone bead
1/2" round wood or goldtone bead
Thick white glue

KNOTS USED
Square Knot
Alternating Square Knots
Berry Knot
Double Half Hitch
Alternating Half Hitches

CUTTING CORDS
Cut twelve 3-yd. cords

INSTRUCTIONS
1. Thread oval bead to center of 4 cords. You will work necklace (up to fastener) in one direction from bead, then in the opposition direction from bead. Follow Fig. 1.
2. On one side of bead, tie a Square Knot. (If hole in bead is so large that the Square Knot will slip into it, tie an Overhand Knot with all cords before tying the Square Knot.)
3. Add a cord to the 2 cords on the left by tying a Square Knot onto these with a new cord folded in center. Repeat on right 2 cords. There are now 8 working cords.
4. Add a new cord to the 2 outer cords on the left with a Square Knot. Repeat on right. There are now 12 working cords.
5. Tie 2 rows of Alternating Square Knots (2-knot row, then 3-knot row).
6. Tie a row of 2 Alternating Square Knots.
7. Tie an Alternating Square Knot with center 4 cords.
8. Using far left cord as holding cord, tie Double Half Hitches diagonally down to center with the left half of cords. Repeat from right. At center, Double Half Hitch the 2 holding cords together.
9. Repeat step 8.
10. Tie a Square Knot with the 4 cords on far left and another with the 4 cords on far right. Tie a row of 2 Alternating Square Knots. Tie a row of 3 Alternating Square Knots.
11. Tie a row of 2 Alternating Square Knots, then tie an Alternating Square Knot with center 4 cords.
12. Using center 2 cords as holding cords, tie Double Half Hitches diagonally down to outside on each side.
13. Repeat step 12.

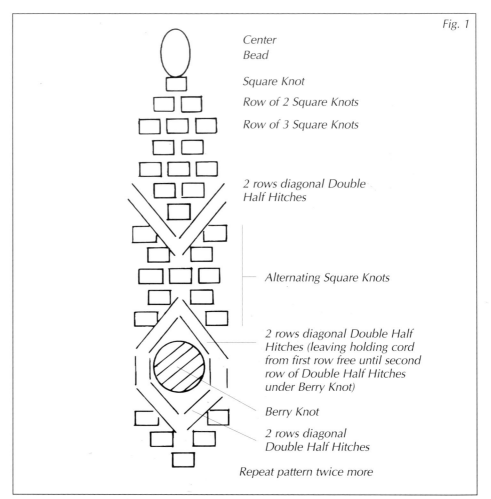

Fig. 1

Center Bead

Square Knot

Row of 2 Square Knots

Row of 3 Square Knots

2 rows diagonal Double Half Hitches

Alternating Square Knots

2 rows diagonal Double Half Hitches (leaving holding cord from first row free until second row of Double Half Hitches under Berry Knot)

Berry Knot

2 rows diagonal Double Half Hitches

Repeat pattern twice more

14. Tie a Berry Knot with center 8 cords, starting and ending with 2 side-by-side Square Knots.
15. Using second cord from the left as holding cord (holding cord from previous Double Half Hitch row), tie Double Half Hitches with left half of cords diagonally down to center. Repeat on right. Double Half Hitch the 2 holding cords together at center.
16. Using far left and far right cords as holding cords, repeat step 15.
17. Repeat steps 10-16 twice.
18. Repeat step 10. If you need to lengthen necklace, add additional rows of Alternating Square Knots at this point, ending with a 2-knot row.
19. Tie an Alternating Square Knot with center 4 cords.
20. Repeat step 8 three times.
21. On both ends of necklace: Glue the 4 cords on left and on right to backside of necklace with thick white glue. When dry, clip excess cord. This leaves 4 working cords in center.
22. Loop end: Divide cords into 2 groups of 2 cords each. Tie a 3/4" chain of Alternating Half Hitches with each group. Tie all 4 cords together with an Overhand Knot. Add glue to knot. When dry, clip cords short.
23. Bead end: Thread the 4 cords through the 1/2" bead. Tie all 4 cords together with an Overhand Knot. Add glue to knot. When dry, clip cords short.

Designed by Sylvia Carroll

Treasured Amber Necklace

Finished length: 24" (end to end)

MATERIALS
16 yds. of 1mm dark natural hemp cord
Five round amber beads, 1/2" diam.
Nine round amber beads, 3/8" diam.

KNOTS USED
Square Knot
Alternating Square Knots

CUTTING CORDS
Cut eight 2-yd. cords.

INSTRUCTIONS
1. Follow Fig. 1. Align 4 cords. String 5 amber beads to center of these 4 cords, alternating a 1/2", 3/8", 1/2", 3/8", 1/2" bead.
2. Tie 3 Square Knots on each side of beads.
3. Align the 4 other cords. Starting at center of them, tie 6 Square Knots in one direction, then 6 Square Knots in the other direction (12 centered Square Knots).

Work the following steps, up to end closure steps, on each side of necklace.

4. Join separate sections by tying a Square Knot with 2 inner cords from each section.
5. Tie 5 rows of Alternating Square Knots.
6. Tie 16 Square Knots with the outside 4 cords (those farthest from neck).
7. Tie a Square Knot with cords of the inside section; slip on 3 beads—a 3/8", a 1/2", then a 3/8"— and tie one Square Knot after the beads.
8. Repeat steps 4 and 5.
9. Separate cords into 4 inside and 4 outside cord groups. Tie a 6 Square Knot sinnet with the outside group.
10. Tie one Square Knot with the inside group. Slip on a 3/8" bead and tie one Square Knot after the bead.
11. Repeat steps 4 and 5.
12. Separate the groups. Tie a 6 Square Knot sinnet with the outside group.
13. Tie a 5 Square Knot sinnet with the inside group.
14. Using the 2 longest cords as knotting cords, tie a 3 Square Knot sinnet around the rest of the cords.
15. Clip the 2 shortest filler cords close to the last Square Knot.
16. Tie 4 Square Knots.
17. Repeat steps 15.
18. Tie 6 square knots.
19. Bead end: At one end of necklace, thread all cords through bead. Bring cords back around bead and tie a Square Knot around end of necklace. Put glue on knot. When dry, cut excess cordage.
20. Loop end: At other end, use longest cord to wrap all other cords for 2". Bend wrapped section into a loop back to end of necklace. Tie a Square Knot around end of necklace. Put glue on knot. When dry, cut excess cordage. ◇

Designed by Kathryn Gould

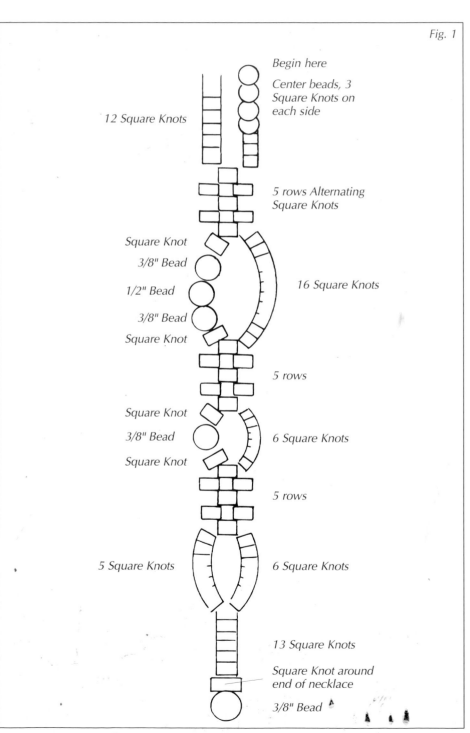

Fig. 1

Begin here

Center beads, 3 Square Knots on each side

12 Square Knots

5 rows Alternating Square Knots

Square Knot
3/8" Bead
1/2" Bead
3/8" Bead
Square Knot

16 Square Knots

5 rows

Square Knot
3/8" Bead
Square Knot

6 Square Knots

5 rows

5 Square Knots

6 Square Knots

13 Square Knots

Square Knot around end of necklace

3/8" Bead

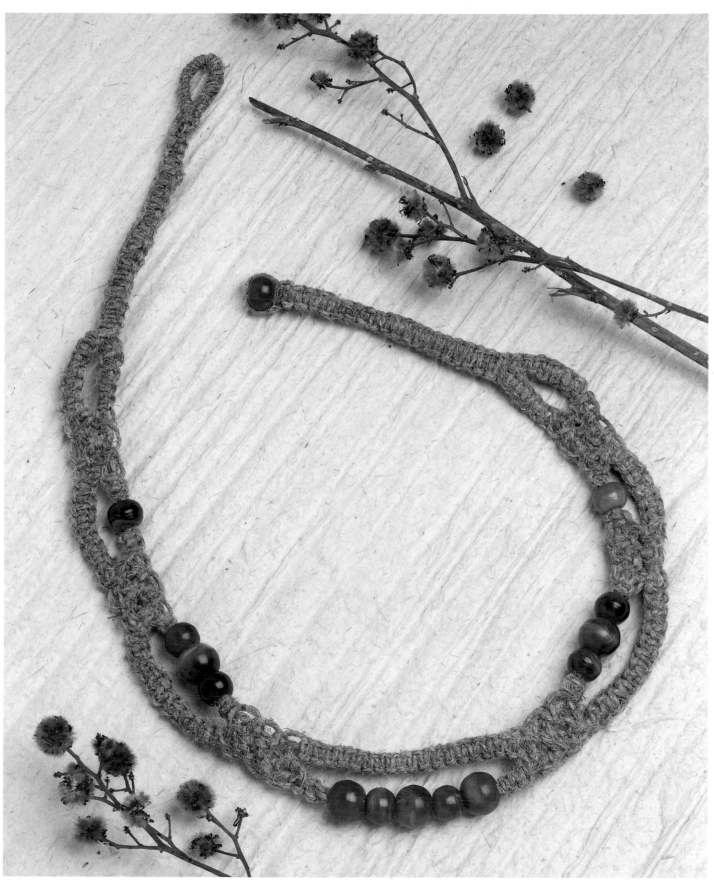

Wrist & Necklace Watches

LACE AND LINES WRIST WATCH

Finished length: Approx. 8" (end to end) Add or subtract rows of Alternating Square Knots to change size.

MATERIALS
4 yds. 1mm dk. natural hemp cord
24" of 1mm red hemp cord
Watch face, 7/8" diam.
Clasp set (such as circle and bar)
Thick white glue

KNOTS USED
Lark's Heads
Square Knot
Alternating Square Knots

CUTTING CORDS
Cut six 24" natural cords.
Cut two 12" red cords.

INSTRUCTIONS
1. Follow Fig. 1. Work each step on one side of watch face, then repeat it on other side of watch face. Mount 3 folded cords to bar of watch face with Lark's Heads.
2. Tie 15 rows of Alternating Square Knots. Use 3 cords per knot for 2-knot rows and the 4 center cords for 1-knot rows. Start and end with a 2-knot row.
3. Tie a Square Knot using 2 knotting cords on each side (4 total) around center 2 cords.
4. Work this step with each red cord on each side of watch face. Fold red cord in half and use as a double cord. With ends on backside of

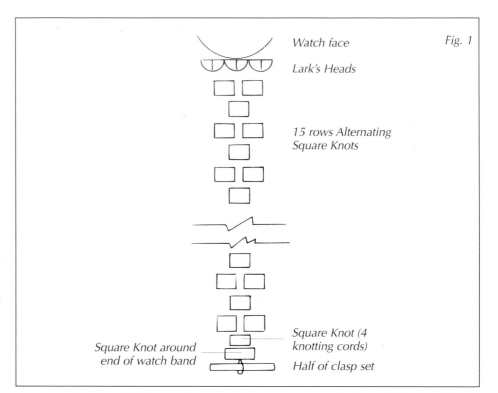

Watch face   Fig. 1

Lark's Heads

15 rows Alternating
Square Knots

Square Knot around   Square Knot (4
end of watch band   knotting cords)

                            Half of clasp set

watch band with filler cords, weave red double cord over and under the center Square Knots (single knot rows) of watch band. Glue red cord ends on backside and let dry.

5. Thread filler cords through one half of clasp set and fold back onto end of watch band. Tie a Square Knot around end of watch band with previous 4 knotting cords. Put glue on knot. When dry, clip excess cordage. �

By Marion Brizendine

CAT TOY NECKLACE WATCH

Finished length: 19-1/2" (ends to end of pendant area)

MATERIALS
14 yds. 1mm orange hemp cord
1 yd. each color 1mm hemp cord: red, yellow, turquoise, brown
Watch face, 1-1/4" diam.
Curved clay tube bead, 2" long
Approx. 22 assorted plastic and metal beads and buttons; include a 1"
tube bead (cat face is a button)

KNOTS USED
Lark's Head
Wrap Knot
Double Half Hitch
Square Knot
Half Knot

Overhand Knot

CUTTING CORDS
Cut four 1-yd. orange cords.
Cut five 2-yd. orange cords.
Cut other colors of cord as needed to lengths needed.

Continued on page 46

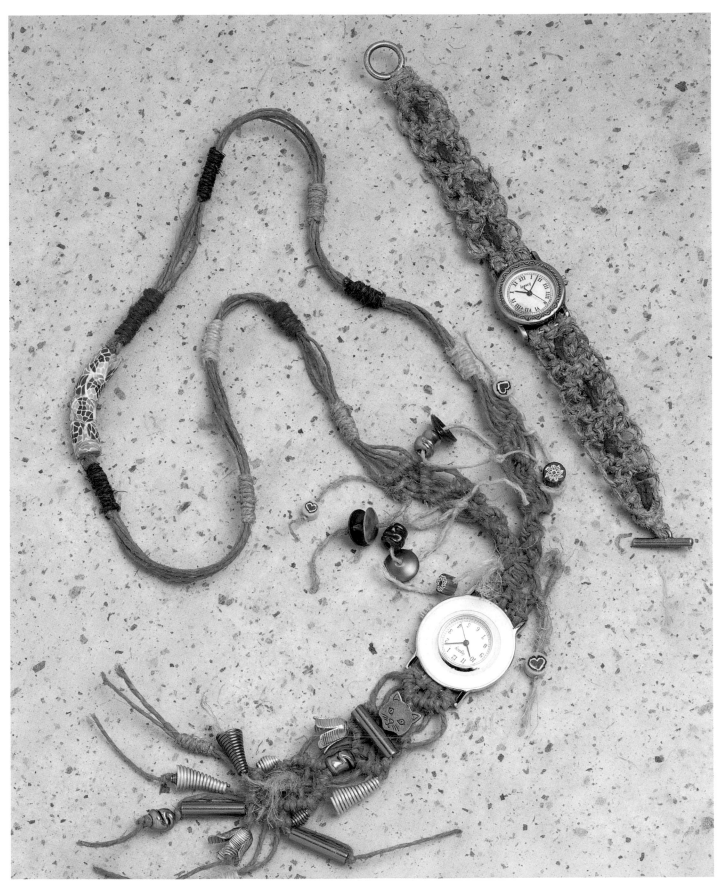

Wrist & Necklace Watches

CAT TOY NECKLACE WATCH

Finished length: 19-1/2" (ends to end of pendant area)

Continued from page 44

INSTRUCTIONS

Dangle Section (below watch)

1. Follow Fig. 1. Attach four 1-yd. cords to top bar of watch face with Lark's Heads. (The watch will be upside down only to a person looking at the wearer, not for the wearer.)
2. Using the outside cord on each side as a holding cord, tie diagonal Double Half Hitches down to the center. Double Half Hitch holding cords together.
3. Add cat face button to the holding cords.
4. Using same holding cords (at center), tie diagonal Double Half Hitches down to the outsides.
5. Thread the 2 holding cords through the 1" tube bead from opposite directions. This positions the bead horizontally.
6. Repeat step 2.
7. Add various beads on the vertical cords.
8. Repeat step 4.
9. Weave the Double Half Hitched cords across each other diagonally, then repeat step 2.
10. Add a bead on each holding cord and repeat step 2 again.
11. String beads on some cord ends and tie Overhand Knots under the beads. Wrap some cord ends with 1/2" Wrap Knots, using various contrasting color cords.

Top of Necklace

1. Follow Fig. 2. Attach five 2-yd. cords to other bar of watch face with Lark's Heads.
2. Tie a row of 2 Square Knots, omitting center 2 cords.
3. Tie a 2 Square Knot sinnet with center 4 cords.
4. Using 3 filler cords in each, tie a 1" sinnet of Half Knots with the left 5 cords and with the right 5 cords.
5. Using inside cord as holding cord, tie Double Half Hitches diagonally down to the outside. Continue with same holding cord and tie Double Half Hitches diagonally down to the inside. With same holding cord, tie Double Half Hitches diagonally down to the outside. Repeat with the other 5 cords of necklace.
6. Skip 1".
7. Tie a 1" Wrap Knot around each 5-cord group with contrasting color cord.
8. Skip 2".
9. Repeat step 7, step 8, and step 7.
10. Skip 3".
11. Repeat step 7 and step 10.
12. Thread 2 cords from one side of necklace through the 2" curved tube bead. Thread 2 cords from other side through same bead in opposite direction. Using contrasting color cord, tie a Wrap Knot around all cords close to end of bead on each side. Clip excess cordage close to bead and close to ends of Wrap Knots.
13. Using contrasting color cords, tie remaining beads to necklace here and there in open work areas. ◇

By Marion Brizendine

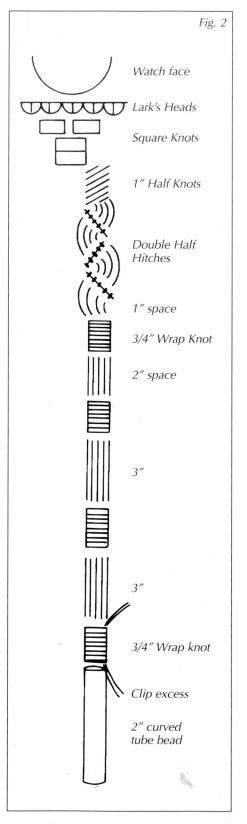

Fig. 2

Watch face
Lark's Heads
Square Knots
1" Half Knots
Double Half Hitches
1" space
3/4" Wrap Knot
2" space
3"
3"
3/4" Wrap knot
Clip excess
2" curved tube bead

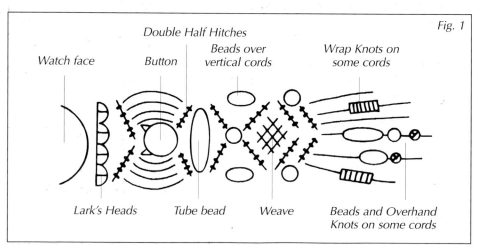

Fig. 1

Double Half Hitches
Watch face
Button
Beads over vertical cords
Wrap Knots on some cords
Lark's Heads
Tube bead
Weave
Beads and Overhand Knots on some cords

46

Bracelets of Green

BEADS IN THE WEAVE

Pictured center on page 49
Finished length: 7-1/2" (end to end) + ties

MATERIALS
6 yds. of 1mm natural color hemp cord
Three 1" round glass beads, 2 light green and one royal blue
Thick white glue

KNOTS USED
Overhand Knot
Weaving To Points On Right & Left Sides
Three-Part Flat Braid

CUTTING CORDS
Cut three 2-yd. cords.

INSTRUCTIONS
1. Follow Fig. 1. Fold the 3 cords in half. At 3/4" from fold, tie an Overhand Knot with all cords, forming a 3/4" loop. There are 6 working cords.

2. Weave 3 cords back and forth over 3 stationary cords, weaving to points. This creates a zigzag shape. Weave for 2".
3. Thread stationary cords through a green bead. Weave for 3/4"
4. Repeat step 3 with a blue bead.
5. Add remaining green bead and weave for 3".
6. Tie an Overhand Knot with alll cords.
7. Divide cords into 2 groups of 3 cords each. Braid each group for 2" to 3" with a Three-Part Flat Braid. Tie an Overhand Knot with all 3 cords together at end of each group. Add glue to Overhand Knots. When dry, cut cords close to knots. Tie braids through loop to fasten necklace. ◈

Designed by Miche Baskett

SHADY GARDEN

Pictured bottom on page 49
Finished length: Approx. 9" (end to end)

MATERIALS
6 yds. 1mm olive green hemp cord
Clay cylinder bead, antiqued ivory with green glaze design, 5/8" long
Four green disc beads, 1/4" wide
Green leaf shape flat end bead, 5/8" long
Thick white glue

KNOTS USED
Half Knot
Square Knot

CUTTING CORDS
Cut four 1-1/2-yd. cords.

INSTRUCTIONS
1. Align the 4 cords. String cylinder bead onto all 4 cords and position it in center. Work each step from bead in both directions to end closure steps.

2. Tie 4 Half Knots.
3. Add a disk bead to filler cords.
4. Tie 10 Half Knots.
5. Add a disk bead to filler cords.
6. Tie Half Knots for 2-1/2" to 3" more.
7. Loop end: Using longest working cord, wrap other cords for 1-1/4". Fold wrapped area in a loop back onto end of bracelet. Tie 2 Square Knots around end of bracelet. Add glue to last knot. When dry, clip excess cordage.
8. Bead end: Thread all cords through leaf shape bead and bring back to end of necklace. Tie 2 Square Knots around end of bracelet. Add glue to last knot. When dry, clip excess cordage. ◈

By Marion Brizendine

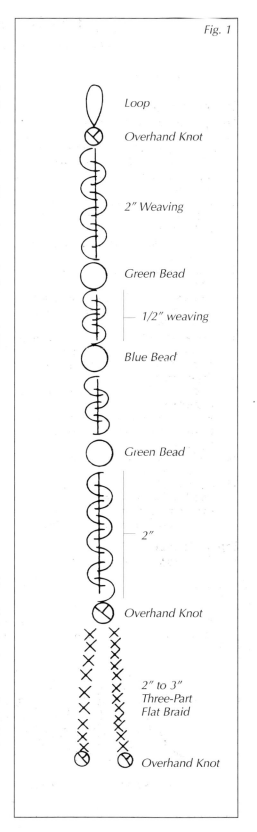

Fig. 1

Loop

Overhand Knot

2" Weaving

Green Bead

1/2" weaving

Blue Bead

Green Bead

2"

Overhand Knot

2" to 3"
Three-Part
Flat Braid

Overhand Knot

Bracelets of Green

STONES IN THE GLADE

Pictured top on page 49
Finished length: Approx. 8" (end to end)

MATERIALS
10 yds. 1mm dk. green hemp cord
Three rough clay cylinder beads, natural and green design, approx. 1/4" long
Thick white glue

KNOTS USED
Square Knot
Chinese Crown Knot

CUTTING CORDS
Cut eight 1-1/4-yd. cords.

INSTRUCTIONS
1. Follow Fig. 1. Align all cords and find the center.
2. Tie an equal number of Chinese Crown Knots for 1-1/2" in each direction from center (3" total).
3. Tie 3 Square Knots (6 filler cords) in each direction.
4. Put a bead on the center 2 cords (on each end of bracelet).
5. Tie a 6-Square-Knot sinnet with the 3 cords on one side of bead. Repeat on other side. Work this step on both ends of bracelet.
6. Tie 2 Square Knots with all cords (6 filler cords) on each end of bracelet. (The previous separate sinnets will curve around bead.)
7. Clip the 2 shortest filler cords and repeat step 6.
8. Loop end: Using longest cord, wrap other cords for 1-1/2". Fold wrapped section back to end of bracelet, forming a loop. Tie a Square Knot around end of bracelet. Put glue on knot. When dry, clip excess cordage.
9. Bead end: Thread cords through remaining bead. Bring them back around bead to end of bracelet. Tie a Square Knot around end of bracelet. Put glue on knot. When dry, clip excess cordage. ◇

Designed by Kathryn Gould

Fig. 1

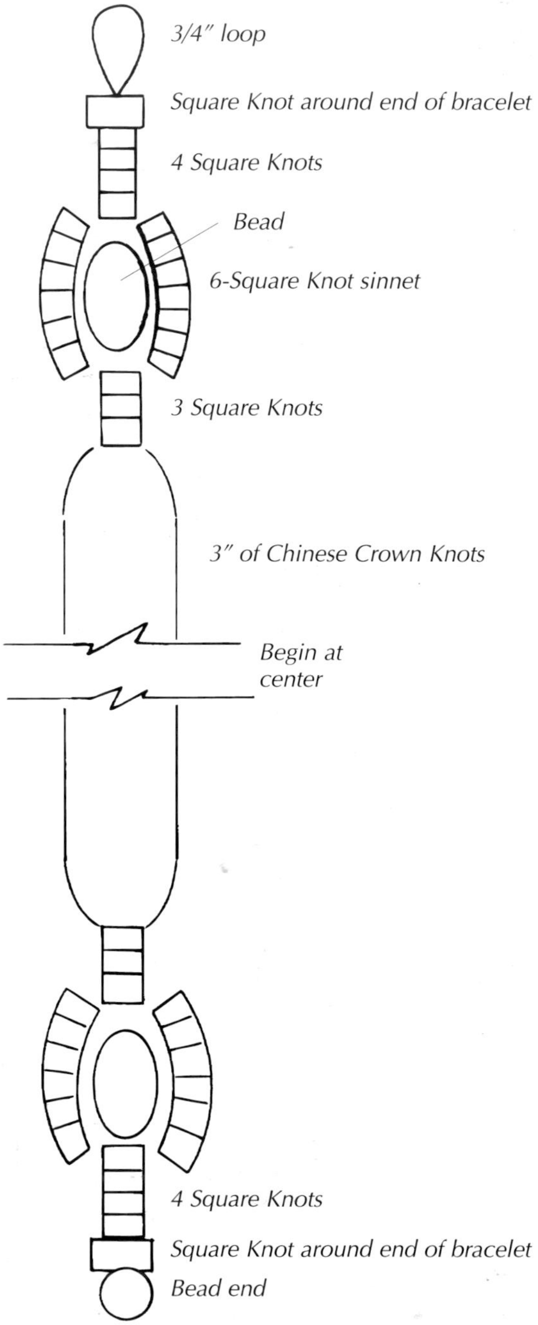

3/4" loop
Square Knot around end of bracelet
4 Square Knots
Bead
6-Square Knot sinnet
3 Square Knots
3" of Chinese Crown Knots
Begin at center
4 Square Knots
Square Knot around end of bracelet
Bead end

Summer Charm Choker

Finished length: 17-1/2" (end to end)

MATERIALS
30 yds. orange 1mm hemp cord
Multi-color ceramic cylindrical bead, 1/2" long
Pony beads—2 deep yellow, 2 medium green
Round wood bead, 1/2" diam.
Thick white glue

KNOTS USED
Square Knot
Alternating Square Knots
Overhand Knot

CUTTING CORDS
Cut twelve 2-1/2-yd. cords.

INSTRUCTIONS
1. Align 4 cords and string cylinder bead to center of all 4 together.
2. Tie 5 Square Knots on each side of bead.
3. Beginning at center of 4 other cords, tie 6 Square Knots in one direction and 7 Square Knots in the other direction (a total of 13 knots). With sinnets placed horizontally, place this sinnet above the sinnet with bead (Fig. 1).
4. Beginning at center of remaining 4 cords, tie 8 Square Knots in one direction and 9 Square Knots in other direction (total of 17). Place this sinnet below the sinnet with bead (Fig. 1).

Work steps 5-17 on both sides of necklace (in both directions from center). Follow Fig. 2.

5. Join the sinnets with Alternating Square Knots.
6. Tie 6 rows of Alternating Square Knots.
7. Tie 3 Square Knots with the 3 outer cords (outside of necklace). Tie 3 Square Knots with the 3 inner cords (inside of necklace). Six center cords are left untied.
8. Place a yellow pony bead on the 2

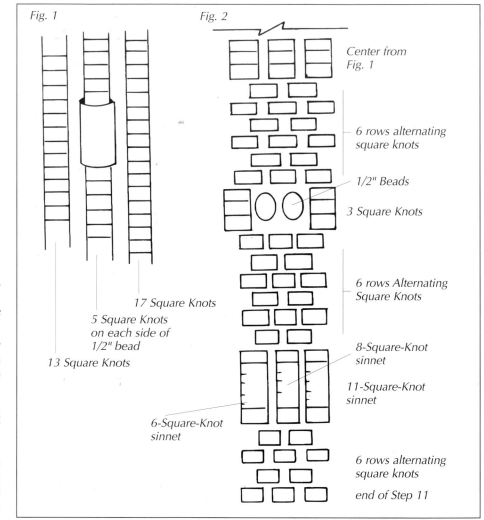

Fig. 1
Fig. 2

Center from Fig. 1

6 rows alternating square knots

1/2" Beads

3 Square Knots

6 rows Alternating Square Knots

8-Square-Knot sinnet

11-Square-Knot sinnet

6-Square-Knot sinnet

6 rows alternating square knots

end of Step 11

17 Square Knots

5 Square Knots on each side of 1/2" bead

13 Square Knots

cords next to inside sinnet. Place a green pony bead on the two cords next to the outside sinnet. (There will be 2 cords between the beads.)
9. Tie 6 rows of Alternating Square Knots, starting with a 3-knot row.
10. Tie an 11-Square-Knot sinnet with the 4 outer cords. Tie an 8-Square-Knot sinnet with the 4 center cords. Tie a 6-Square-Knot sinnet with the 4 inner cords.
11. Tie 6 rows of Alternating Square Knots.

12. Divide cords into 2 groups of 6 cords each. Using the 2 longest cords in each group as knotting cords, tie 10 Square Knots with each group (use 4 filler cords).
13. Using all cords, tie 3 Square Knots (with 2 knotting cords and 4 filler cords); then clip the 2 shortest filler cords.
14. Repeat step 13 two more times for a total of 9 Square Knots.
15. Continue tying Square Knots until desired length is reached.

Continued on page 52

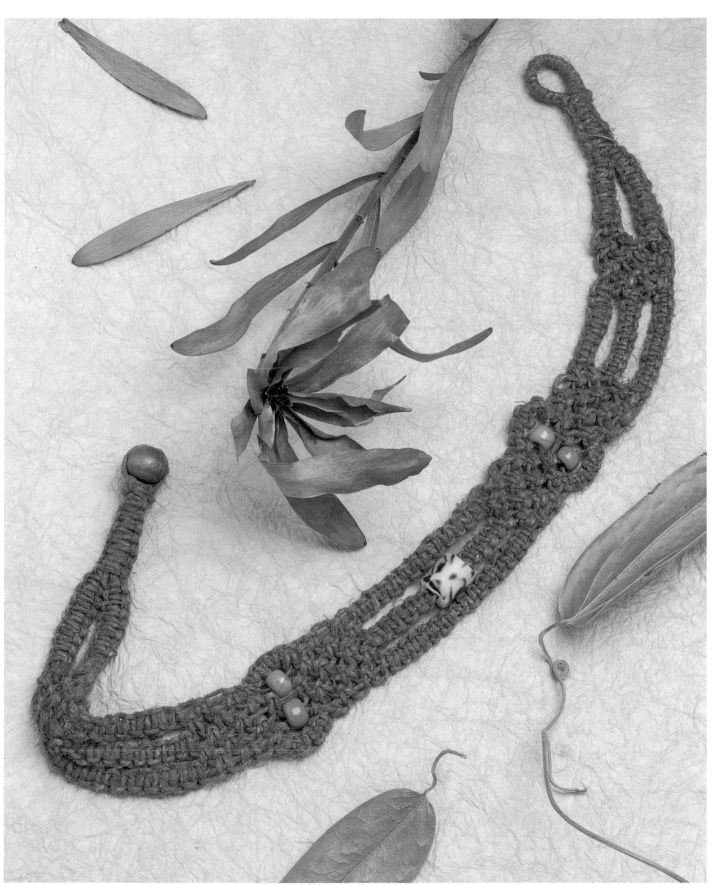

Summer Charm Choker

Continued from page 50

Finished length: 17-1/2″ (end to end)

16. Work a bead ending on one side of necklace: Pull all cords through the round bead. Bring cords around outside of bead and tie a Square Knot next to the bead over end of necklace. Tie an Overhand Knot over the Square Knot. Clip cords close to knot and secure with glue.

17. Create a wrapped loop ending on other end of necklace: Use longest working cord to wrap all other cords, beginning at last knot. Wrap until there is enough length to form a loop that will accommodate the end bead on other side of necklace. Loop wrapped section back around to the end of necklace. Separate the cords and tie a Square Knot around the knots at end of necklace. With the 2 outside cords, tie an Overhand Knot over the Square Knot. Clip cords close and add a drop of glue to knot. ◫

Designed by Kathryn Gould

Ebony & Ivory

DARK SAFARI CHOKER

Pictured at left of page 53
Finished length: 16″ (end to end)

MATERIALS
6-1/4 yds. 1mm black hemp
Ceramic beads—two 5/8″ ovals, one 1/2″ round
Six goldtone bells, 1/4″ diam.
Black shank button, 1/2″ wide
Thick white glue

KNOTS USED
Overhand Knot
Square Knot

CUTTING CORDS
Cut one 5-yd. cord.
Cut one 45″ cord.

INSTRUCTIONS
1. Align cords and fold in half. Tie cords together with an Overhand Knot, leaving a 1/2″ loop.
2. Tie 5″ of Square Knots.
3. Thread filler cords through an oval bead.
4. Tie 7 Square Knots, adding a bell to *right* knotting cord on every other knot (3 bells).
5. Thread filler cords through round bead.
6. Tie 7 Square Knots, adding a bell to *right* knotting cord on every other knot (3 bells).
7. Thread filler cords through an oval bead.
8. Tie 5″ of Square Knots.
9. Tie a black shank button on center cords. Tie all cords together with a Square Knot (use 4 knotting cords, no fillers). Apply a dot of thick white glue to ending knot. Clip ends. ◫

Designed by Patti Cox

More instructions on page 54.

53

Ebony & Ivory

Oriental Pendant

Pictured on right of page 53

Finished length: 14-1/2" (from ends to center) + pendant

MATERIALS

10-1/2 yds. 1mm black hemp cord
Chinese ivory-look pendant
Three oval beads with large holes, 5/8" long
Four round ivory-look beads, 3/16" diam.
Two round black beads, 1/4" diam.
Thick white glue

KNOTS USED

Lark's Head
Square Knot
Half Knot
Overhand Knot

CUTTING CORDS

Cut one 3-yd. cord.
Cut three 2-yd. cords.
Cut cords for Wrap Knots to lengths needed as you need them.

INSTRUCTIONS

1. Attach the 3-yd. cord to the pendant with a Lark's Head. There are 2 working cords.
2. Fold a 2-yd. cord in half and attach with a Lark's Head to each working cord. There are now 6 working cords. Divide into two 3-cord groups (2 knotting cords and 1 filler cord per group.)

Work steps 3-8 on both sides of necklace, referring to Fig. 1.

3. Tie 7 Square Knots. Add an oval bead on all 3 cords together.
4. Tie 6 Half Knots. Add a small ivory bead on filler cord.
5. Repeat step 4, then tie 6 more Half Knots.
6. Skip 1" and tie 2 Square Knots. Repeat twice more.
7. Thread all 3 cords through a black bead.
8. Skip 1/2" and tie a 1/2" Wrap Knot around all 3 cords. Repeat twice.
9. Loop end: After last space, wrap around the 3 cords for 2-1/4". Loop wrapped section back to end of necklace. Tie 2 Square Knots and one Overhand Knot around end of bracelet. Put glue on Overhand Knot. When dry, clip excess cordage.
10. Bead end: Thread all 3 cords through an oval bead. Bring cords back around bead to end of necklace. Tie 2 Square Knots and one Overhand Knot around end of bracelet. Put glue on Overhand Knot. When dry, clip excess cordage. ◇

By Marion Brizendine

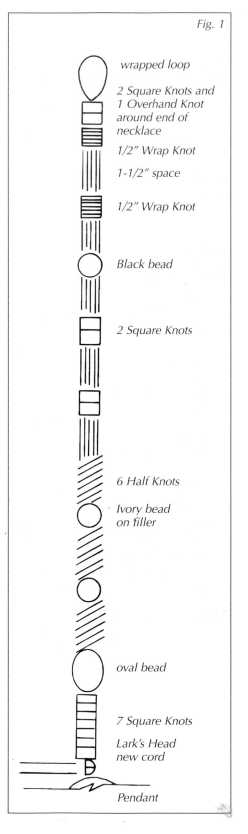

Fig. 1

wrapped loop

2 Square Knots and 1 Overhand Knot around end of necklace

1/2" Wrap Knot

1-1/2" space

1/2" Wrap Knot

Black bead

2 Square Knots

6 Half Knots

Ivory bead on filler

oval bead

7 Square Knots

Lark's Head new cord

Pendant

Millefiori Twist

Finished length: 18" (end to end)

MATERIALS
5 yds. + 45" of 1mm natural color hemp
Three 1" long cylindrical millefiori beads
Round black shank button, 1/2" wide
Thick white glue

KNOTS USED
Overhand Knot
Half Knot
Square Knot (no fillers)

CUTTING
Cut one 5-yd. cord
Cut one 45" cord

INSTRUCTIONS
1. Fold the cords in half to find and align centers.
2. Tie cords together at center with an Overhand Knot, leaving a 1/2" loop. You will have 2 center (filler) cords and 2 knotting cords.
3. Tie 5" of Half Knots.
4. Thread centers cords through a bead.
5. Tie 1" of Half Knots.
6. Thread center cords through a bead.
7. Tie 1" of Half Knots.
8. Thread center cords through a bead.
9. Tie 5" of Half Knots.
10. Tie a black shank button on center cords. Tie all cords together with a Square Knot (use 4 knotting cords, no fillers). Apply a dot of thick white glue to ending knot. Clip ends. ◊

Designed by Patti Cox

Love & Peace

Finished length: 14" (from ends to bottom of cross)

MATERIALS
30-1/2 yds. 1mm dk. natural hemp cord
Four brass spacer type beads, 1/4" wide
One round wood bead, 3/8" diam.
Thick white glue

KNOTS USED
Lark's Head
Square Knot
Alternating Square Knots
Double Half Hitch

CUTTING CORDS
Necklace Area:
Cut one 3/4-yd. cord
Cut two 1-3/4-yd. cords.
Cross Pendant:
Cut four 3-1/2-yd. cords.
Cut eight 1-1/2-yd. cords

INSTRUCTIONS
Cross:
1. Follow Fig 1. Fold the four 3-1/2-yd. cords in half and mount with Lark's Heads to the center of the 3/4-yd. cord. This gives 8 working cords for the cross. (Keep holding cord ends up out of the way.)
2. Tie 10 rows of Alternating Square Knots, starting with a 2-knot row.
3. Left horizontal arm: Fold four 1-1/2-yd. cords and mount with Lark's Heads to the second working cord (from left) of the vertical arm. This provides 8 working cords that are perpendicular to previous cords. With these cords, tie 6 rows of Alternating Square Knots, starting with a 2-knot row. String a brass bead onto center 2 working cords. Continue Alternating Square Knot pattern for 7 more rows, ending with a 2-knot row. Pull cord 1 horizontally across other cords for a holding cord. Double Half Hitch other cords onto it. Cut cords to 1/4" long. Turn and glue ends to backside of horizontal cross arm.
4. Right horizontal arm: Mount four 1-1/2-yd. cords onto vertical cord 7 (second cord from right). Repeat step 3 with these 8 working cords.
5. Remainder of vertical arm: Thread a brass bead onto center 2 cords. Tie a Square Knot directly under bead with the center 4 cords. (This is the first row of an Alternating Square Knot pattern.) Continue Alternating Square Knot pattern for 6 more rows, ending with a 1-knot row.. Put a bead on center 2 cords. Tie 7 more rows of Alternating Square

Knots, ending with a 2-knot row. Using cord 1 as a holding cord, Double Half Hitch other cords onto it. Cut cords to 1/4" long. Turn and glue ends to backside of vertical arm.

Necklace Section:
Follow Fig. 2. Work these steps on both sides of necklace.
1. Fold a 1-3/4-yd. cord in half and attach with a Square Knot to holding cord next to original Lark's Heads.
2. Tie a sinnet of 5 Square Knots (1 filler cord).
3. Skip 3/8" and tie a Square Knot. Skip 3/8" and tie a Square Knot. Skip 3/8".
4. Repeat steps 2 and 3 until side of necklace is 7" long.

Closure:
1. Loop end: Wrap one cord with the other for 1-1/2". Loop wrapped section back to end of necklace. Tie an Overhand Knot around end of bracelet. Put glue on knot. When dry, clip excess cordage.
2. Bead end: Thread cords through round wood bead. Bring cords back around bead to end of necklace. Tie an Overhand Knot around end of bracelet. Put glue on knot. When dry, clip excess cordage. ◇

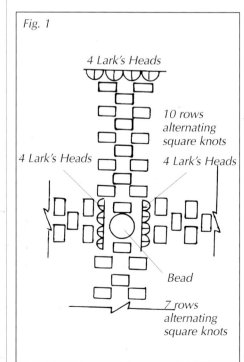

Fig. 1

4 Lark's Heads

10 rows alternating square knots

4 Lark's Heads

4 Lark's Heads

Bead

7 rows alternating square knots

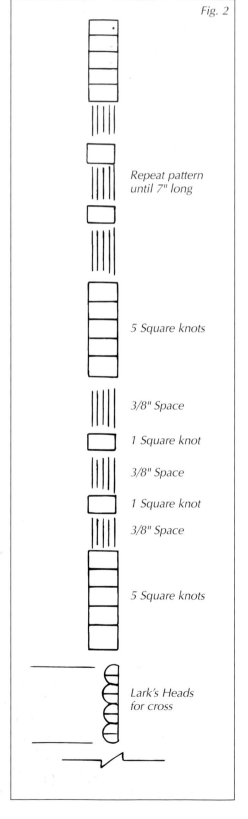

Fig. 2

Repeat pattern until 7" long

5 Square knots

3/8" Space

1 Square knot

3/8" Space

1 Square knot

3/8" Space

5 Square knots

Lark's Heads for cross

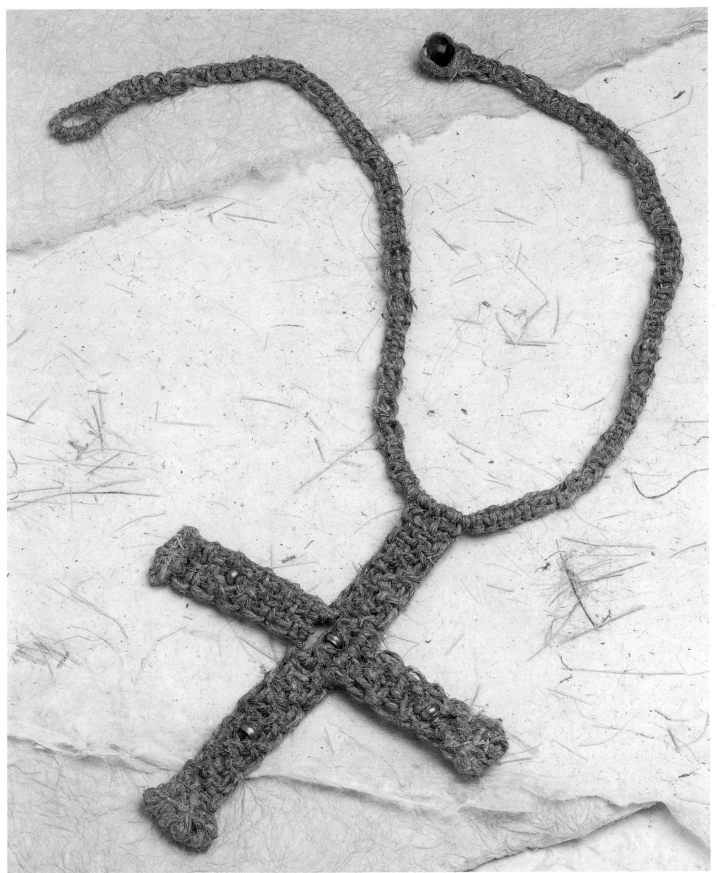

African Amulet

Finished length: 22-1/2" end to end

MATERIALS
22 yds. 1mm dk. green hemp cord
Approx. 28 beads, assorted shapes, colors, and sizes (1/2" to 3/4")
Optional: 2 or more eye pins

KNOTS USED
Square Knot
Lark's Head
Alternating Square Knots
Overhand Knot

CUTTING CORDS
Cut one 5-yd. cord.
Cut 17, 1-yd. cords.

INSTRUCTIONS
One Side of Necklace Area:
1. Follow Fig. 1. Fold the 5-yd. cord in half. Fold three 1-yd. cords together in half and place fold 1" from fold of 5-yd. cord to leave a loop at end of necklace. All folded cords create 8 working cords.
2. Using the longer cords as knotting cords, tie 5 Square Knots around 6 filler cords. Skip 1-1/4" and tie 5 Square Knots. Repeat until you have a total of 5 Square-Knot-sections.

This side of necklace will be approximately 10" long.

Amulet Section:
1. Follow Fig. 2. Fold 14, 1-yd. cords in half and mount to all 8 necklace cords (as one) with Lark's Heads. This creates 28 working cords for amulet section.
2. Tie 8 rows of Alternating Square Knots. Start with a 7-knot row. Tie 5 more decreasing rows of Alternating Square Knots (dropping one Square Knot on each side per row), ending with one center Square Knot.
3. String beads at various lengths on cord ends and tie an Overhand Knot under each bead. Cut cord ends to 1/4"-1/2" below beads. If desired, attach some beads to cords in Alternating Square Knot section with eye pins.

Other Side of Necklace:
1. Repeat step 2 for other side of necklace, working pattern in reverse.
2. Tie cord ends into 2 Overhand Knots, one on top of the other. Cut cords 1/4" from knot. ◇

Designed by Sandy Dye

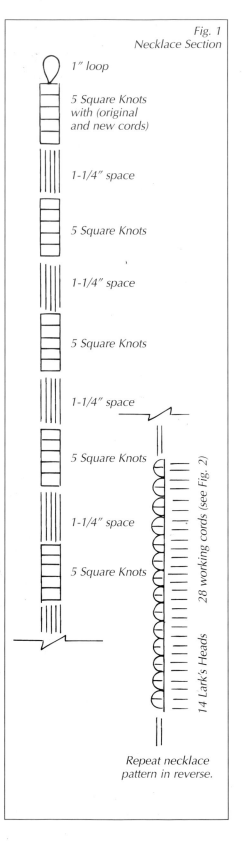

Fig. 1
Necklace Section

1" loop

5 Square Knots with (original and new cords)

1-1/4" space

5 Square Knots

1-1/4" space

5 Square Knots

1-1/4" space

5 Square Knots

1-1/4" space

5 Square Knots

28 working cords (see Fig. 2)

14 Lark's Heads

Repeat necklace pattern in reverse.

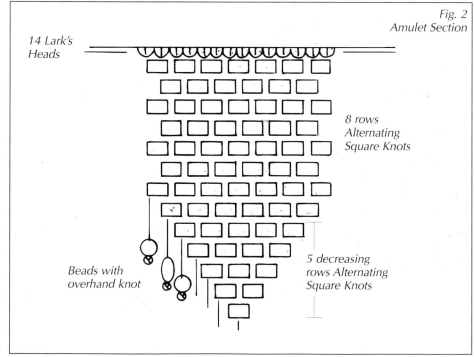

Fig. 2
Amulet Section

14 Lark's Heads

8 rows Alternating Square Knots

5 decreasing rows Alternating Square Knots

Beads with overhand knot

59

Fish On a String

Finished length: 18-1/2" (from ends to bottom of pendant)

MATERIALS
13-1/3 yds. 1mm natural-color hemp
Ceramic fish pendant, 2" long
Ceramic cylindrical beads, 1/4" long—
 4 brown, 2 peach
Thick white glue

KNOTS USED
Lark's Head
Josephine Knot
Square Knot
Half Hitch Spiral
Overhand Knot

CUTTING CORDS
Cut four 3-1/3-yd. cords.

INSTRUCTIONS
1. Fold all 4 cords at center and mount through hole of pendant bead with a Lark's Head. There are 8 working cords. Follow Fig. 1.
2. Skip 1-1/4" and tie a Josephine Knot with all 8 cords. Skip 1" and tie another Josephine Knot with all 8 cords.
3. Divide cords into 2 groups of 4 cords each. Work steps 4-9 with each group.
4. Skip 1/4" and tie a Square Knot. Thread filler cords through a brown bead. Tie a Square Knot close under bead.
5. Repeat step 4 with a peach bead.
6. Repeat step 4 (brown bead)
7. Skip 1/2" and tie a Josephine Knot.
8. Repeat step 7 seven times.
9. Skip 1/2" space, then tie a 3" long Half Hitch Spiral.
10. With one 4-cord group, divide cords into 2 groups of 2 cords each. With each 2-cord group, tie a 1" long Half Hitch Spiral. Bring all 4 cords together and tie an Overhand Knot. Cut excess off cords and add glue to Overhand Knot. Fig. 2.
11. With other 4-cord group, tie a large Overhand Knot with all cords. Cut excess off cords and add glue to Overhand Knot. Fig. 3. ◇

Designed by Miche Baskett

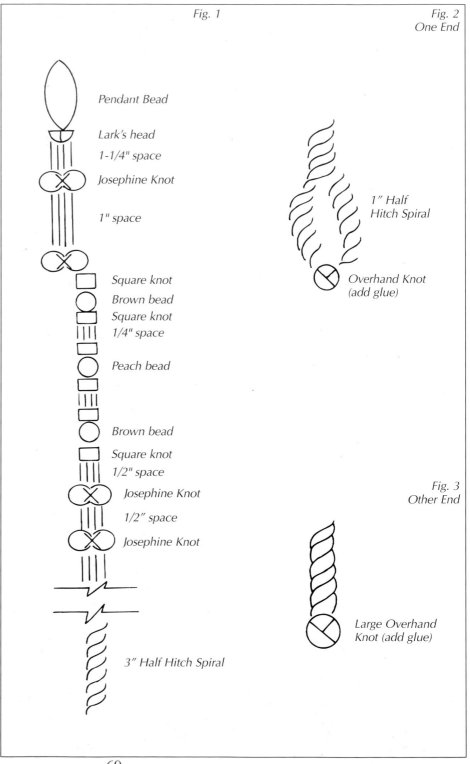

Fig. 1

Pendant Bead

Lark's head
1-1/4" space

Josephine Knot

1" space

Square knot
Brown bead
Square knot
1/4" space

Peach bead

Brown bead
Square knot
1/2" space

Josephine Knot

1/2" space

Josephine Knot

3" Half Hitch Spiral

Fig. 2
One End

1" Half Hitch Spiral

Overhand Knot
(add glue)

Fig. 3
Other End

Large Overhand Knot (add glue)

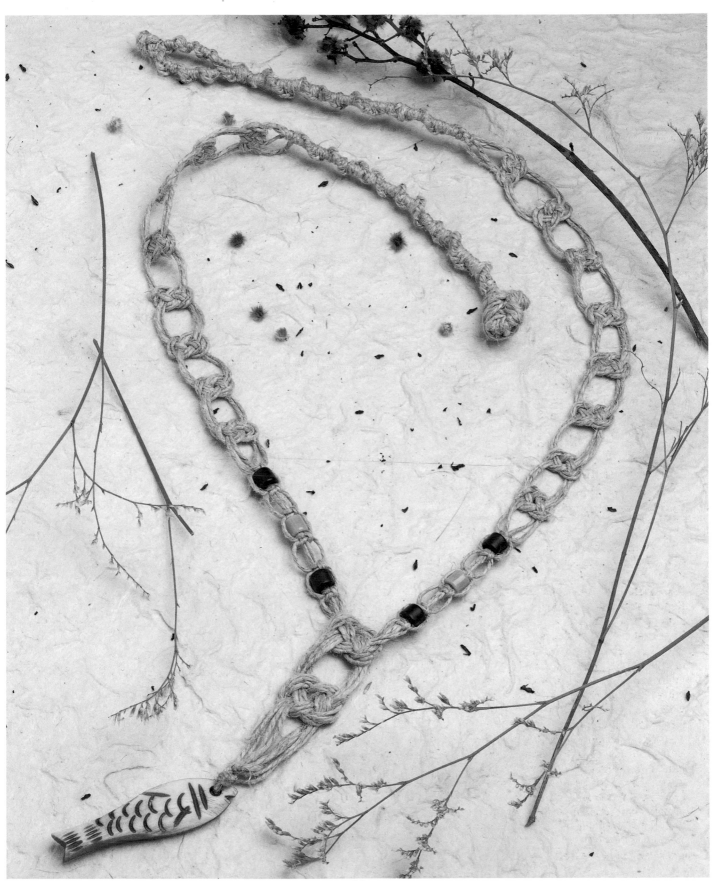

Purple Passion

Finished length: 12-1/2" (from ends to center of bead)

MATERIALS

14 yds. 1mm purple hemp cord
Transparent amethyst cylinder bead, 1" long
Round wood bead, 3/8" diam.
Thick white glue

KNOTS USED

Square Knot
Half Knot
Double Half Hitch

CUTTING CORDS

Cut six 2-1/3-yd. cords

INSTRUCTIONS

1. Follow Fig. 1. String bead to center of all 6 cords.
2. Tie 8 Square Knots on each side of beads, using 4 filler cords.
3. Form a circle with knotted sections and join them by tying 2 Square Knots with the center 4 cords.
4. Tie 3 Square Knots with the 4 cords on each side of step 3.
5. Divide cords in half. Use the inner cord (inside of necklace) as a holding cord. Double Half Hitch the other 5 cords in each group diagonally up from center of necklace to outside.
6. Repeat step 5. Do not Double Half Hitch the holding cords from previous row.
7. Repeat step 6 until there are 5 rows of Double Half Hitches forming a "triangle." Repeat steps 5-7 on other side, then tie a Half Knot with the 2 inner cords to attach both triangles together.

Steps 8-25 are given for only one side of necklace. As you complete each step, repeat it on other side of necklace.

8. Use the inside cord as a holding cord and Double Half Hitch all other 5 cords in a diagonal line down to the outside of necklace.
9. Repeat step 8. Do not Double Half Hitch the holding cord from previous row.
10. Repeat step 9 until there are 5 rows of Double Half Hitches forming a "triangle."
11. Use the same cord used as holding cord in step 8 as the holding cord and Double Half Hitch all other 5 cords along the "outside" of the triangle, in a straight line (see Fig. 2).
12. Continue to use the same holding cord and Double Half Hitch the first outer cord (the cord which was used as holding cord in step 9) in a looping fashion. (Loop this cord down and back up to Double Half Hitch it where step 11 ended. Use a T-pin to help hold the shape of each loop as you Double Half Hitch the cord to the holding cord.) Repeat with other cords. You should have 5 loops.

13. Repeat step 12, looping toward the inside of necklace—looping up and back down to the holding cord. Begin these Double Half Hitches where step 12 ended.
14. Repeat step 13 on the outside of necklace (as in step 12).
15. Use the first inner cord as a holding cord and Double Half Hitch all other cords *except* the holding cord from the previous row (the holding cord of steps 12, 13, and 14).
16. Repeat step 15 until you have formed a "triangle." (Do not Double Half Hitch holding cords from previous rows when doing each subsequent row.)
17. Tie 9 Square Knots with the 3 cords on the outside of necklace.
18. Tie 9 Square Knots with the 3 cords on the inside of necklace.
19. Tie 2 Square Knots around 4 cords.
20. Tie 9 Square Knots with the 3 inside cords.
21. Tie 9 Square Knots with the 3 inside cords.
22. Tie 30 Square Knots using 4 filler cords. If more length is desired, tie more Square Knots.
23. Cut the 2 shortest cords and tie 4 Square Knots around the 2 remaining cords.
24. Cut the 2 filler cords.
25. Loop end: Wrap one cord with the other for 1-1/2". Bend the wrapped section into a loop back to end of necklace. Tie a Square Knot around end of necklace. Put glue on knot. When dry, clip off excess cordage.
26. Bead end: Thread cords through round wood bead. Bring cords around bead back to end of necklace. Tie a Square Knot around end of necklace. Put glue

on knot. When dry, clip off excess cordage. ◇

Designed by Kathryn Gould

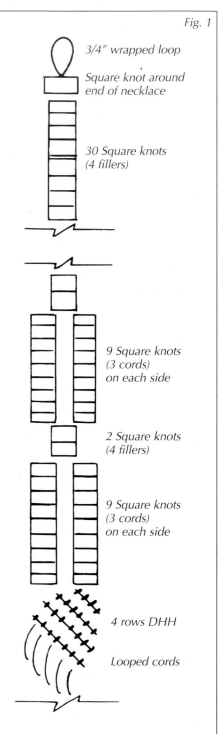

Fig. 1

3/4" wrapped loop

Square knot around end of necklace

30 Square knots (4 fillers)

9 Square knots (3 cords) on each side

2 Square knots (4 fillers)

9 Square knots (3 cords) on each side

4 rows DHH

Looped cords

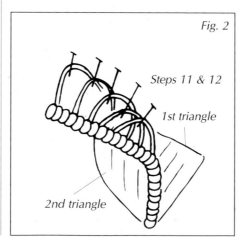

Fig. 2

Steps 11 & 12

1st triangle

2nd triangle

Berry Knot & Bobble Chokers

BERRY KNOTS AND BEADS CHOKER

Finished length: 15 (end to end)

MATERIALS
6-2/3 yds. 1mm natural-color hemp cord
Five ivory cylindrical beads, 3/4" long
Wood shank button, 1/2"
Thick white glue

CUTTING CORDS
Cut four 1-2/3-yd. cords

KNOTS USED
Overhand Knot
Square Knot (with and without fillers)
Berry Knot

INSTRUCTIONS
1. Fold the 4 cords in half to find and align centers.
2. Tie all an Overhand Knot with all cords, leaving a 1/2" loop. There are 8 working cords. Follow Fig. 1 as you work.
3. Tie 5 Berry Knots, ending each with a row of 2 Square Knots pulled tightly.
4. Thread the 2 center cords through a bead. Tie a row of 2 Square Knots close to bead. Tie a Berry Knot, ending it with 2 tight Square Knots.
5. Repeat step 4 three more times.
6. Thread the 2 center cords through a bead. Tie a row of 2 Square Knots close to bead.
7. Tie 5 Berry Knots, ending each with a row of 2 tight Square Knots.
8. If additional length is needed, separate the 8 cords into 2 groups of 4 cords each. Tie a sinnet of Square Knots with each group until you have the additional length you need. Bring all 8 cords together and tie 2 Square Knots, using 4 filler cords and 4 knotting cords (2 knotting cords on each side).
9. Tie a wood shank button on center 4 cords. Tie all cords together with a Square Knot (use 8 knotting cords, no fillers). Apply a dot of thick white glue to ending knot. Clip ends. ◇

Designed by Patti Cox

Additional project instructions on page 66

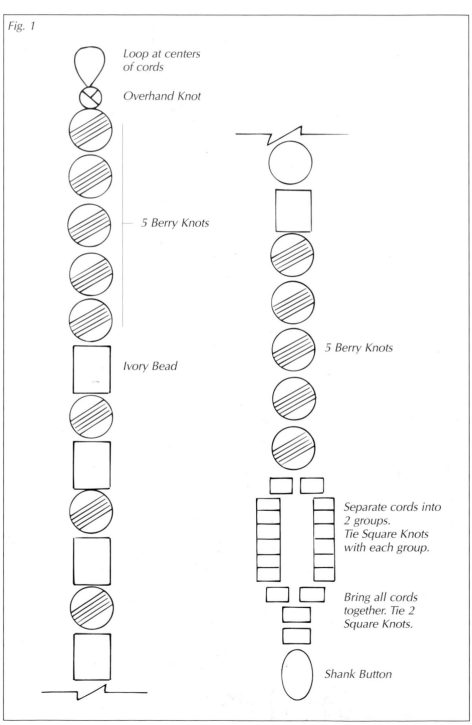

Fig. 1

Loop at centers of cords

Overhand Knot

5 Berry Knots

Ivory Bead

5 Berry Knots

Separate cords into 2 groups.
Tie Square Knots with each group.

Bring all cords together. Tie 2 Square Knots.

Shank Button

Berry Knot & Bobble Chokers

LACE 'N BOBBLES CHOKER

Pictured right on page 65
Finished length: 16" (end to end)

MATERIALS
6-2/3 yds. 1mm natural-color hemp
1/2" brown shank button
Thick white glue

KNOTS USED
Overhand Knot
Alternating Square Knots
Square Knot Bobbles
Square Knot (no fillers)

CUTTING CORDS
Cut four 1-2/3-yd. cords

INSTRUCTIONS
1. Fold the 4 cords in half to find and align centers.
2. Tie an Overhand Knot with all cords, leaving a 1/2" loop. There are 8 working cords. Follow Fig. 1 as you work.
3. Tie 5-1/2" of Alternating Square Knots, starting and ending with a 2-knot row.
4. Tie a Square Knot Bobble consisting of 4 Square Knots with center 4 cords.
5. Tie 1" (approximately 5 rows) of Alternating Square Knots, starting and ending with a 2-knot row.
6. Tie a Square Knot Bobble consisting of 4 Square Knots with center 4 cords.
7. Tie 1" (approximately 5 rows) of Alternating Square Knots, starting and ending with a 2-knot row.
8. Tie a Square Knot Bobble consisting of 4 Square Knots with center 4 cords.
9. Tie 5-1/2" of Alternating Square Knots, starting and ending with a 2-knot row.
10. Tie a brown shank button on center 4 cords. Tie all cords together with a Square Knot (use 8 knotting cords, no fillers). Apply a dot of thick white glue to ending knot. Clip ends. ⊠

Designed by Patti Cox

Fig. 1

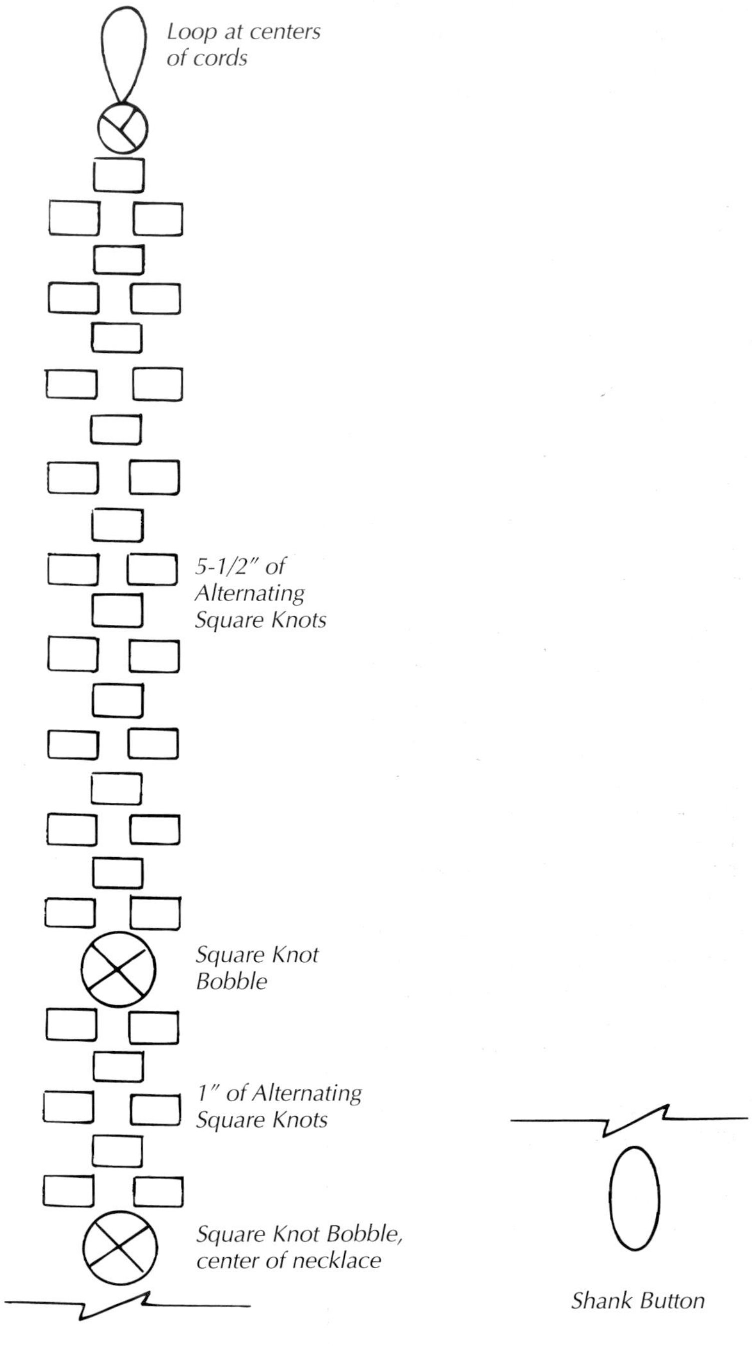

Loop at centers of cords

5-1/2" of Alternating Square Knots

Square Knot Bobble

1" of Alternating Square Knots

Square Knot Bobble, center of necklace

Shank Button

The Moon & Stars

STARS AND FLOWERS CHOKER

Pictured right on page 69

Finished length: 14-1/4" (end to end). To lengthen or shorten, tie more or fewer Half Knots on each end.

MATERIALS

12 yds. 1mm natural-color hemp cord
Two brown wood pony beads, 3/8" or
    8mm wide
One Millefiori flat square bead with
    stars and flowers, 5/8" wide

KNOTS USED

Overhand Knot
Half Knot
Alternating Square Knots

CUTTING CORDS

Cut four 3-yd. cords.

INSTRUCTIONS

1. Align all cords and fold in half. At 3/4" from fold, tie an Overhand Knot. This creates a loop and 8 working cords. Follow Fig. 1 as you work.
2. Tie a Square Knot using 4 knotting cords and 4 filler cords.
3. Tie a 3-1/4" sinnet of Half Knots.
4. Tie 8 rows of Alternating Square Knots, starting with a 2-knot row.
5. Tie a 3/4" Half Knot sinnet with the left 4 cords and another with the right 4 cords.
6. Tie a Square Knot with the center 4 cords.
7. String a pony bead on the 2 center cords.
8. Tie 3 rows of Alternating Square Knots, starting with a 2-knot row.
9. String the Millefiori bead onto center 4 cords. This is center of necklace.
10. Repeat steps 8, 7, 6, 5, and 4 in that order.
11. Tie 2 Overhand Knots with all cords. Trim cords. ◇

Designed by Janet Zielke

Fig. 1

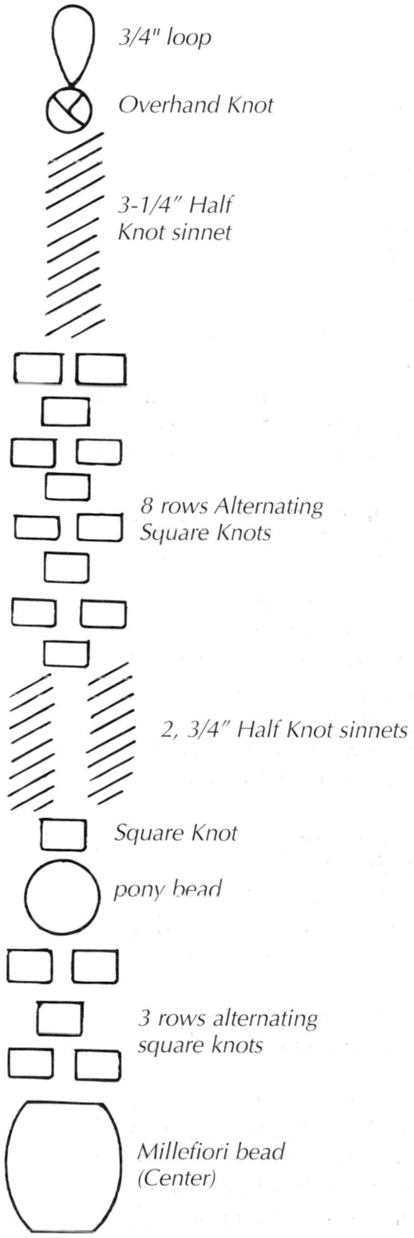

3/4" loop

Overhand Knot

3-1/4" Half
Knot sinnet

8 rows Alternating
Square Knots

2, 3/4" Half Knot sinnets

Square Knot

pony bead

3 rows alternating
square knots

Millefiori bead
(Center)

The Moon & Stars

MOON CHARM NECKLACE

Pictured left on page 69
Finished length: 14-1/2" (from ends to bottom of moon)

MATERIALS
6 yds. 1mm dk. natural hemp cord
Two brown round wood beads, 3/8" or
8mm diam.
Six round wood disk beads, 3/8" or
8mm wide—4 tan (maple), 2 brown
(walnut)
Moon charm, 7/8" long

KNOTS USED
Overhand Knot
Half Knot

CUTTING CORDS
Cut three 2-yd. cords.

INSTRUCTIONS
1. String moon charm to center of all 3 cords. With cords folded at moon, tie an Overhand Knot with all 6 working cords. Separate cords into 3 for one side of necklace and 3 for other side. Use one filler cord in Half Knots.
    Repeat each step on other side of necklace. Follow Fig. 1 as you work.
2. Skip 3" and tie an Overhand Knot.
3. Tie a 1-1/4" sinnet of Half Knots.
4. String a round bead on filler cord.
5. Repeat step 3.
6. String a tan disk bead on filler cord. Tie a Half Knot. String a brown disk bead on filler. Tie a Half Knot (in opposite direction—the second half of a Square Knot). String a tan bead on filler cord.
7. Tie a 1-1/2" sinnet of Half Knots.
8. Tie an Overhand Knot with all 3 cords.
9. Skip 4-1/2" and tie another Overhand Knot with all 3 cords. Trim cords. ◇

Designed by Janet Zielke

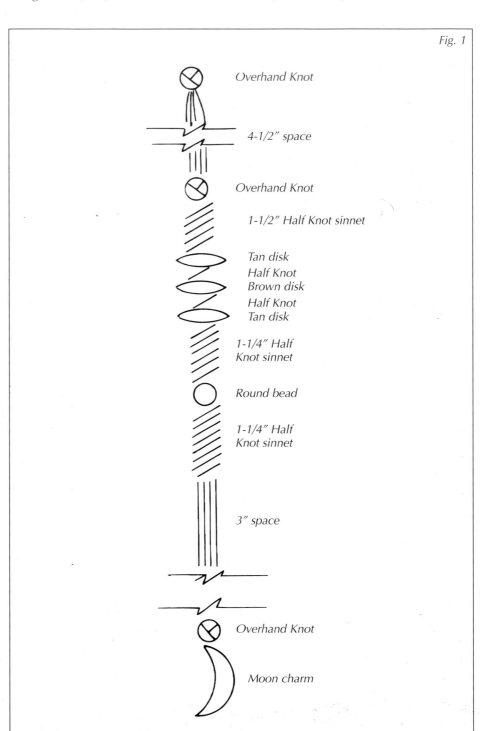

Fig. 1

Overhand Knot

4-1/2" space

Overhand Knot

1-1/2" Half Knot sinnet

Tan disk
Half Knot
Brown disk
Half Knot
Tan disk

1-1/4" Half
Knot sinnet

Round bead

1-1/4" Half
Knot sinnet

3" space

Overhand Knot

Moon charm

Secret Keeper Necklace

Finished length: 13-1/2" (from back of neck to bottom of pouch) + tassel

MATERIALS
38 yds. 1mm dk. natural hemp cord
Thick white glue   *114*

KNOTS USED
Lark's Head
Square Knot
Alternating Square Knot
Half Knot
Overhand Knot
Wrap Knot

CUTTING CORDS
Cut one 7-yd. cord.
Cut 29, 1-yd. cords
Cut eight 6" cords
Cut two 12" cords

INSTRUCTIONS
Pouch:

1. Follow Fig. 1 while working necklace. Fold the 7-yd. cord in half. Use it doubled as a holding cord. Mount 28, 1-yd. cords onto it with Lark's Heads to within 1" of the fold. (The fold will now be a loop.) There are 56 working cords.

2. Tie a row of Square Knots, using 4 cords per knot, starting with the first 4 cords.

3. Tie a row of Alternating Square Knots. This includes tying a Square Knot using the first and last 2 cords which will form your work into a tube. Slip ends of holding cord through loop made by holding cord. Keep holding cord ends up out of the way.

4. Tie 7 more rounds of Alternating Square Knots (total of 9 rounds).

5. With front 28 cords, tie 7 decreasing rows of Alternating Square Knots (drop one knot on each end of each row, ending with one center Square Knot on 7th row). Repeat with the back 28 cords.

6. Place pouch on a flat surface and match up front and back rows. Close sides in V-shaped area by tying a sideways Square Knot with 2 cords from front and 2 from back on each row; do this on left and on right sides of pouch. As you tie each knot, push cord ends to inside and continue to next row. Turn pouch inside out. Glue side closing knots and clip excess cord ends. Turn right side out.

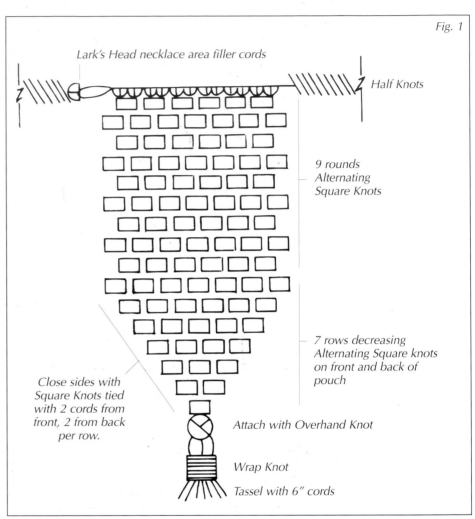

Fig. 1

Lark's Head necklace area filler cords

Half Knots

9 rounds Alternating Square Knots

7 rows decreasing Alternating Square knots on front and back of pouch

Close sides with Square Knots tied with 2 cords from front, 2 from back per row.

Attach with Overhand Knot

Wrap Knot

Tassel with 6" cords

Necklace Area:

1. Fold in half and mount remaining 1-yd. cord to loop of holding cord with a Lark's Head. This will provide filler cords for necklace. The long ends of holding cord will provide the 2 knotting cords. Pull on these knotting cords until loop in holding cord disappears.

2. Tie Half Knots to within 3-1/2" of filler cord ends. Place all cords through pouch around holding cord at point opposite where you began necklace area. Using longest 2 cords as knotting cords, tie Half Knots back to where you left off. Put glue on last knot and cut cord ends.

Tassel:

1. Fold the 6" cords in half. Place a 12" cord through fold. Tie around center of the 6" cords, tying 12" cords in an Overhand Knot.

2. Bring all ends of 6" cords together. Tie a Wrap Knot around all cords near fold with remaining 12" cord. Cut excess ends of wrap cord.

3. Thread cords from Overhand Knot through 2 spaces at bottom point of pouch. Tie these ends in an Overhand Knot on inside of pouch to attach tassel to pouch. Clip excess cord ends.   ◇

Designed by Sandy Dye

Natural Beauties Chokers

CHAIN OF BEADS

Pictured left on page 73
Finished length: 16" (end to end)

MATERIALS
10 yds. 1mm natural-color hemp cord
Eight round antique goldtone beads (more if needed for longer necklace), 3/8" diam.
Eight round antique silvertone beads (more if needed for longer necklace), 3/8" diam.
Round goldtone bead, 1/2" diam.
Thick white glue

KNOTS USED
Alternating Half Hitches
Square Knot

CUTTING CORDS
Cut two 5-yd. cords.

INSTRUCTIONS
1. Place the 2 cords together. Find and align centers.
2. Tie a 1-1/2" chain of Alternating Half Hitches at center. Follow Fig. 1. Fold chain in half to form loop, bringing ends together. There are 4 working cords. Tie a Square Knot.
3. Separate cords into 2 groups of 2 cords each. Tie 5 Alternating Half Hitches with the left 2 cords and 5 Alternating Half Hitches with the right 2 cords.
4. Thread the nearest left cords through a bead. Thread the nearest right cord through same bead in the opposite direction. These 2 cords have now exchanged sides.
5. Repeat step 3. Bring ends of the 2 chained sinnets together and tie a Square Knot with the 4 cords.
6. Repeat steps 3-5 fifteen times (more for a longer necklace), alternating goldtone and silvertone beads.
7. Thread all cords through the 1/2" bead. Bring cords around bead and tie a Square Knot around end of necklace (2 knotting cords on each side). Add glue to this knot. When dry, clip cords short. ◈

Designed by Sylvia Carroll

DESERT TREASURE

Pictured right on page 73
Finished length: 13-1/2" (end to end)

MATERIALS
6-1/4 yds. 1mm natural color hemp
Three turquoise beads, 1/2" wide
Natural wood shank button, 1/2" wide
Thick white glue

KNOTS USED
Overhand Knot
Square Knot (with and without fillers)
Square Knot with Picots

CUTTING
Cut one 5-yd. cord
Cut one 45" cord

INSTRUCTIONS
1. Fold cords in half to find centers. Tie cords together with an Overhand Knot, leaving a 1/2" loop.
2. Tie 3" of Square Knots.
3. Tie 2-1/2" of Square Knots with picot loops every third knot (total of 5 sets of picots).
4. Thread filler cords through a bead.
5. Tie 3 Square Knots, a Square Knot with picots, then 3 more Square Knots.
6. Thread filler cords through a bead.
7. Repeat steps 6-3 (in that order) for other side of necklace.
8. Tie a shank button on center cords. Tie all cords together with a Square Knot (use 4 knotting cords, no fillers). Apply a dot of thick white glue to ending knot. Clip ends. ◈

Designed by Patti Cox

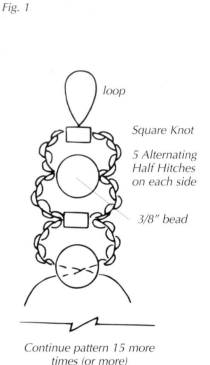

Fig. 1

loop

Square Knot

5 Alternating Half Hitches on each side

3/8" bead

Continue pattern 15 more times (or more)

Square Knot with cords through bead

1/2" bead

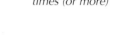

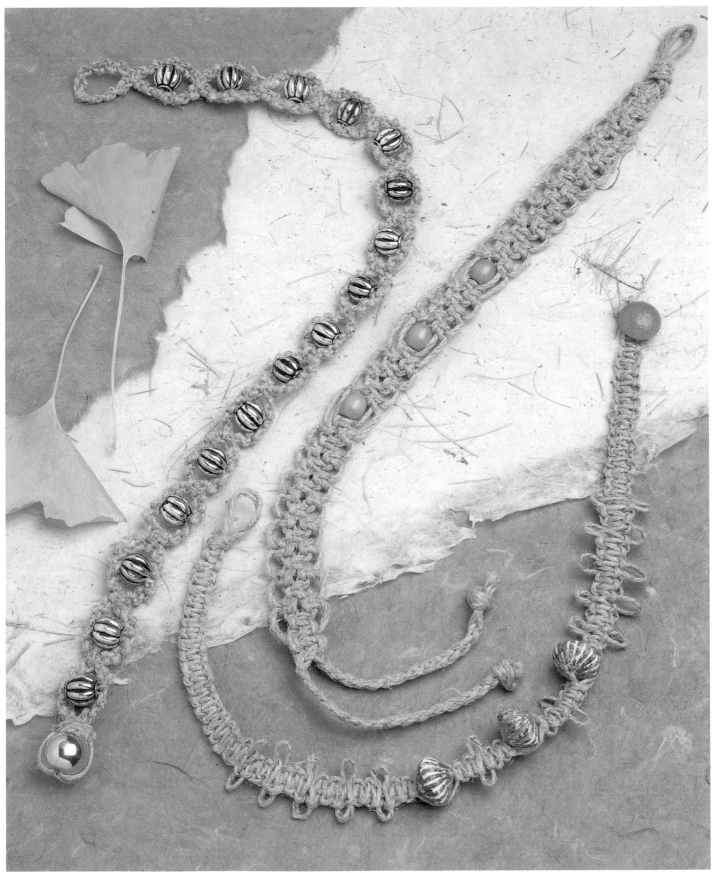

Natural Beauties Chokers

Easy Living

Pictured center on page 73
Finished length: 12" (end to end) + ties

MATERIALS
5-3/4 yds. 1mm natural-color hemp
  cord
Three deep yellow wood oval beads,
  3/8" long

KNOTS USED
Overhand Knot
Square Knot
Three-Part Flat Braid

CUTTING CORDS
Cut three 1-7/8-yd. cords.

INSTRUCTIONS
1. Fold cords to find and align the centers.
2. Tie an Overhand Knot with all cords together, leaving a 3/4" loop. See top of Fig. 1.
3. Tie a Square Knot with all cords using 4 knotting cords and 2 filler cords.
4. Tie a Square Knot with the center 4 cords. Tie a Square Knot with the left 3 cords (one filler cord) and a Square Knot with the right 3 cords (one filler cord). When tying the 2-knot rows, tie knots so that all nubbins are toward center. The nubbin is reversed by reversing the order of the two steps of a Square Knot. Repeat this step for 3-1/2" (approximately 19 rows of Alternating Square Knots).
5. Thread the 2 center cords through a bead.
6. Tie 6 rows of Alternating Square Knots.
7. Repeat steps 5 and 6, then step 5 again.
8. Repeat step 4.
9. Repeat step 3.
10. Divide cords into 2 groups of 3 cords each. Braid cords in each group for 3" using a Three- Part Flat Braid. Tie an Overhand Knot with all cords of the group together. Tie these braids through the loop on other end of choker to fasten choker. ◇

Designed by Miche Baskett

Fig. 1

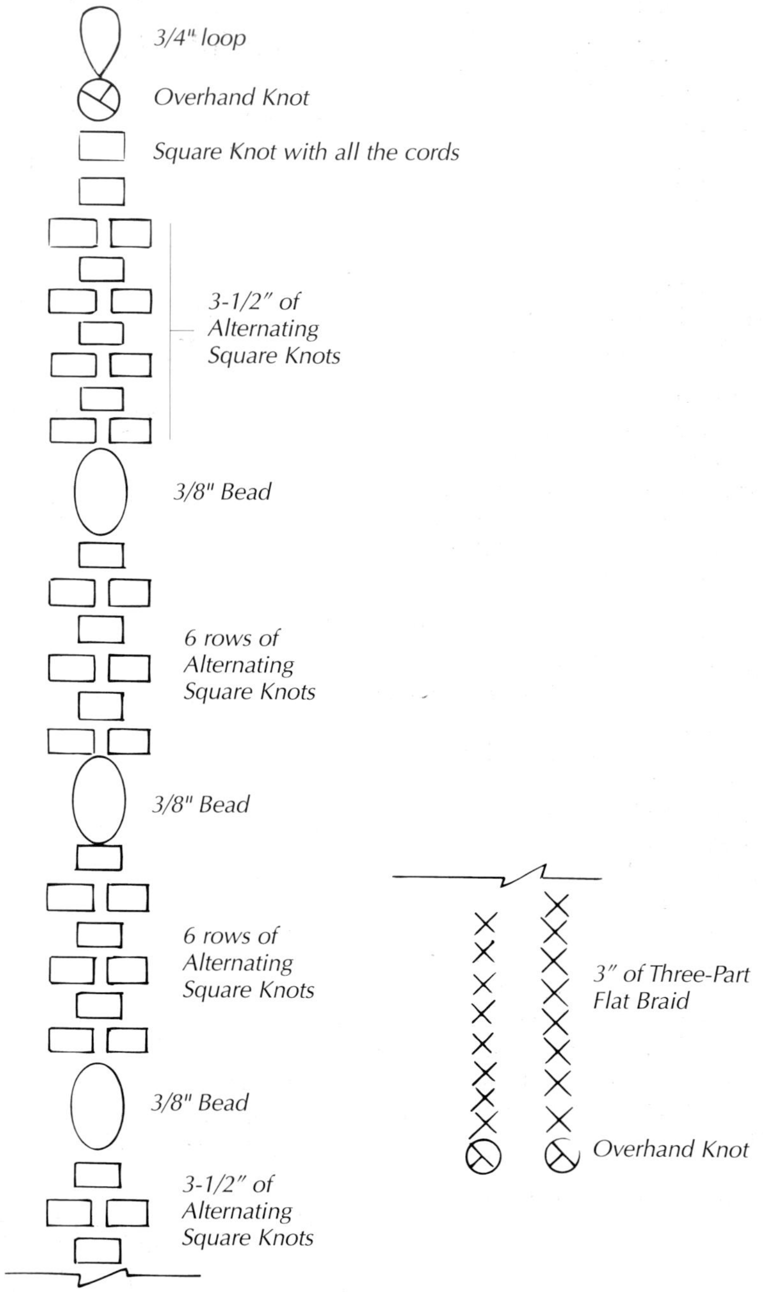

3/4" loop

Overhand Knot

Square Knot with all the cords

3-1/2" of
Alternating
Square Knots

3/8" Bead

6 rows of
Alternating
Square Knots

3/8" Bead

6 rows of
Alternating
Square Knots

3/8" Bead

3-1/2" of
Alternating
Square Knots

3" of Three-Part
Flat Braid

Overhand Knot

Day At the Beach Anklet

Finished length: 9-1/2" (end to end)

MATERIALS
2 yds. 1mm dk. natural hemp cord
1 yd. 1mm turquoise hemp cord
Six transparent turquoise pony beads
  (or similar type 3/8" beads)
Thick white glue

KNOTS USED
Overhand Knot
Square Knot

CUTTING CORDS
Cut two 1-yd. natural cords.
Cut one 1-yd. turquoise cord.

INSTRUCTIONS
1. Align the three cords and tie them together at one end with an Overhand Knot. (The knot will create an "end bead.") Use natural cords for knotting cords and turquoise cord as filler cord throughout anklet..
2. Thread a bead on all 3 cords. Tie a Square knot under bead,
3. Skip 1/4" space on filler cord and tie a Square Knot.
4. Repeat step 3 four more times.
5. Repeat step 2.
6. Repeat step 3 twice.
7. Repeat step 2 three times.
8. Repeat step 3 twice.
9. Repeat step 2.
10. Repeat step 3 six times.
11. Loop end: Wrap natural cords for 2-1/4" with turquoise cord. Fold wrapped section back to end of anklet to form a loop. Tie a Square Knot around end of anklet. Put glue on knot and clip excess cordage.
◇

Designed by Marion Brizendine

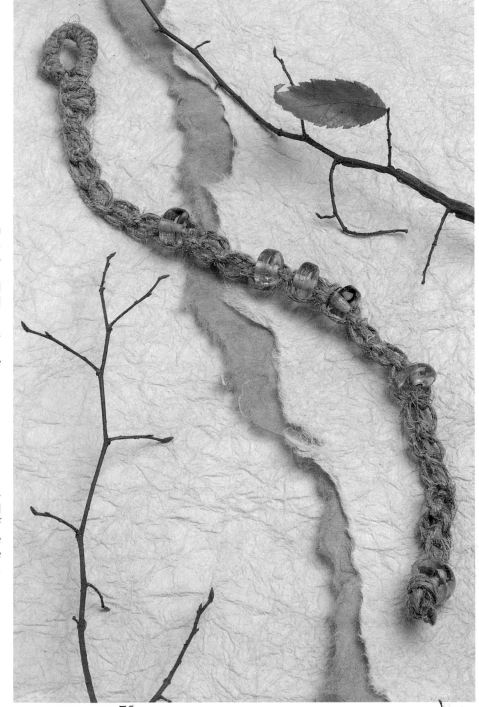

Scallops & Beads Choker

Finished length: 17-1/2 (end to end)

MATERIALS
11-3/4 yds. 1mm natural-color hemp cord
Approx. 13 red round wood beads (more
    for a longer necklace), 1/4" ; hole must
    accommodate at least one cord
Round wood bead, 1/2"
Thick white glue

KNOTS USED
Square Knot
Alternating Half Hitches

CUTTING
Cut two cords 4-1/2 yds. long
Cut one cord 2-3/4 yds. long

INSTRUCTIONS
1. Fold cords to find and align centers. This
    will also form a loop at one end of neck-
    lace. Follow Fig. 1. Drop down 3/4"
    from fold and tie 2 Square Knots using 2
    of the longest cords for knotting cords
    (all others as filler cords). There are 6
    working cords.
2. Arrange cords so that 2 long cords are
    on the outside left and 2 long cords are
    on the outside right. As you knot, make
    sure the long cords continue to end up
    in these positions before tying
    Alternating Half Hitches. You may want
    to mark these cords in some way for
    easy identification.
3. With the 4 cords on the left: Tie 2 Square
    Knots. Thread a bead on at least one
    filler cord (both if the hole in your bead
    will accommodate them). Tie 2 Square
    Knots.
4. With the right 2 cords, tie a chain of 14
    Alternating Half Hitches. Loop the chain
    around to be directly beside the last
    Square Knot tied.
5. With the 4 cords on the right, tie 2
    Square Knots.
6. With the 2 cords on the left, tie a chain
    of 7 Alternating Half Hitches. Loop the
    chain around to be directly beside the
    last Square Knot tied.
7. Repeat steps 3-6 eleven times (more for
    a longer necklace).
8. Repeat steps 3 and 4.
9. Tie 2 or 3 Square Knots with 2 knotting
    cords (one on each outside) and 4 filler
    cords.
10. Thread all cords through the 1/2" bead.
    Bring 2 shorter cords around bead to front
    of necklace and 2 shorter cords around

bead to back of necklace. Bring remaining
two longer cords around bead and tie 2
Square Knots, using the end of necklace
plus the filler cords as filler. Add thick

white glue to these knots. When dry, clip
cord ends short. ◇

Designed by Sylvia Carroll

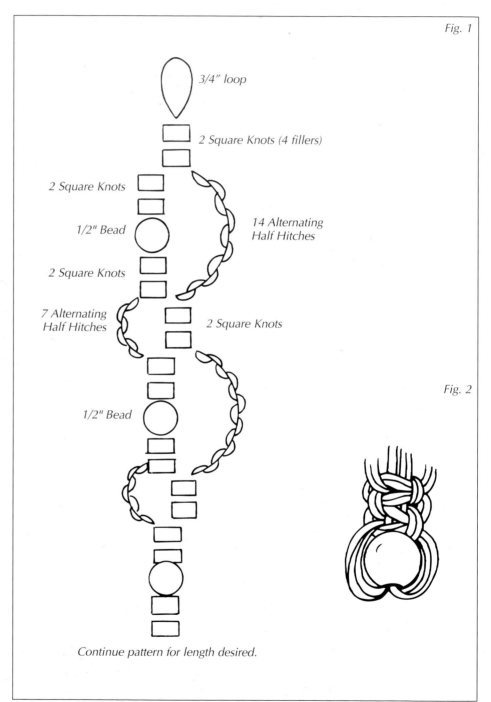

Fig. 1

3/4" loop

2 Square Knots (4 fillers)

2 Square Knots

1/2" Bead

2 Square Knots

14 Alternating
Half Hitches

7 Alternating
Half Hitches

2 Square Knots

1/2" Bead

Fig. 2

Continue pattern for length desired.

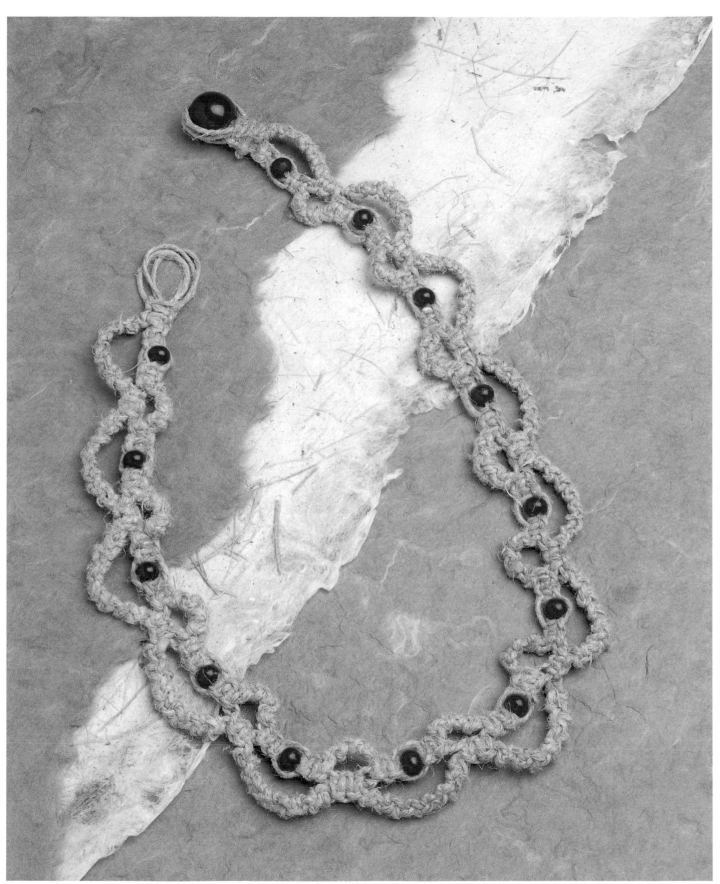

Dancing Dangles

Finished length: 18-1/2" (from ends to bottom of dangles)

MATERIALS
10-1/2 yds.1mm natural-color hemp
2 color striped ceramic cylindrical
 beads, 3/4" long
Ivory-look beads—two 1/4" cylindrical,
 four 1/2" ovals, one 1/2" disk shape
Cobalt blue glass beads—four 3/8" long
 cylindrical, one 3/8" round
Medium blue opaque glass cylinder
 beads, 1/4" long
Glazed pottery canteen shaped (flat
 oval) bead, 3/4" x 1/2"
Thick white glue

KNOTS USED
Overhand Knot
Half Hitch
Square Knot
Lark's Head

CUTTING
2 cords each 12" long
1 cord 6 yds. + 34" long
1 cord 2 yds. + 28" long

INSTRUCTIONS
Left Side:
1. Fold longest 2 cords in half to find and align centers.
2. Tie all cords together with an Overhand Knot, leaving a 3/4" loop. There are 4 working cords.
3. Tie a 1" long Half Hitch sinnet.
4. Tie Square Knots for 1".
5. Tie a 1/2" long Half Hitch sinnet.
6. Skip a 3/4" space and tie 3 Square Knots.
7. Thread a medium blue bead on filler cords. Tie 3 Square Knots starting close to bead.
8. Skip a 3/4" space and tie 3 Square Knots.
9. Tie a 1-1/2" long Half Hitch sinnet..
10. Tie 2 Square Knots. Skip a 1/4" space. Tie 2 Square Knots. Skip another 1/4" space. Tie 2 more Square Knots.
11. Thread filler cords through an ivory oval bead.
12. Repeat step 10.
13. Repeat step 9.
14. Tie 1/2" of Square Knots.
15. Thread a 3/8" cobalt blue cylinder bead on filler cords.

16. Tie 1/2" of Square Knots.
17. Thread a color-striped ceramic bead on filler cords.
18. Repeat steps 14-16.
19. Tie a 1" Half Hitch Spiral.
20. Tie 3 Square Knots.
21. Thread a 1/4" ivory cylinder bead on filler cords.
22. Tie 3 Square Knots.

Dangle:
1. Fold remaining 2 cords in half and attach to filler cords of main necklace with a Lark's Head (Fig. 1). New cords will be perpendicular to cords of main necklace. There are 4 working cords for dangle. Work with these cords in this section of instructions, following Fig. 2.
2. Tie 2 Square Knots.
3. Thread filler cords through canteen shape bead.
4. Tie 2 Square Knots.
5. Tie an Overhand Knot with each outer cord close to Square Knots. Thread an ivory oval bead on each outer cord. Thread a cobalt blue round bead on the 2 center cords. Tie an Overhand Knot at end of the 2 outer cords. Tie one Overhand Knot at end of the 2 center cords together.

Right Side:
1. Repeat necklace pattern in reverse, up *to* the step 3 Half Hitch sinnet (do not do this sinnet).
2. Place disk shape ivory bead on all 4 cords 1" from last Square Knot. Fold cords around bead and tie an Overhand Knot (Fig. 3). Lay cords against each other and trim 3 of the loose cords to 3/4" long. With remaining loose cord, tie a Half Hitch sinnet around all other cords, working back toward last Square Knot. When sinnet meets Square Knots, tie an Overhand Knot with the knotting cord around other cords and trim excess.
3. Place a dot of glue on the Overhand Knot. ◇

Designed by Miche Baskett

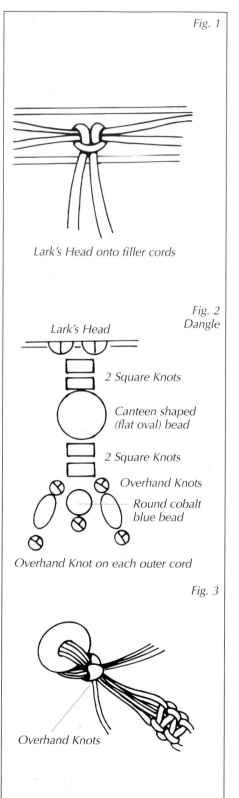

Fig. 1

Lark's Head onto filler cords

Fig. 2
Dangle

Lark's Head
2 Square Knots
Canteen shaped (flat oval) bead
2 Square Knots
Overhand Knots
Round cobalt blue bead

Overhand Knot on each outer cord

Fig. 3

Overhand Knots

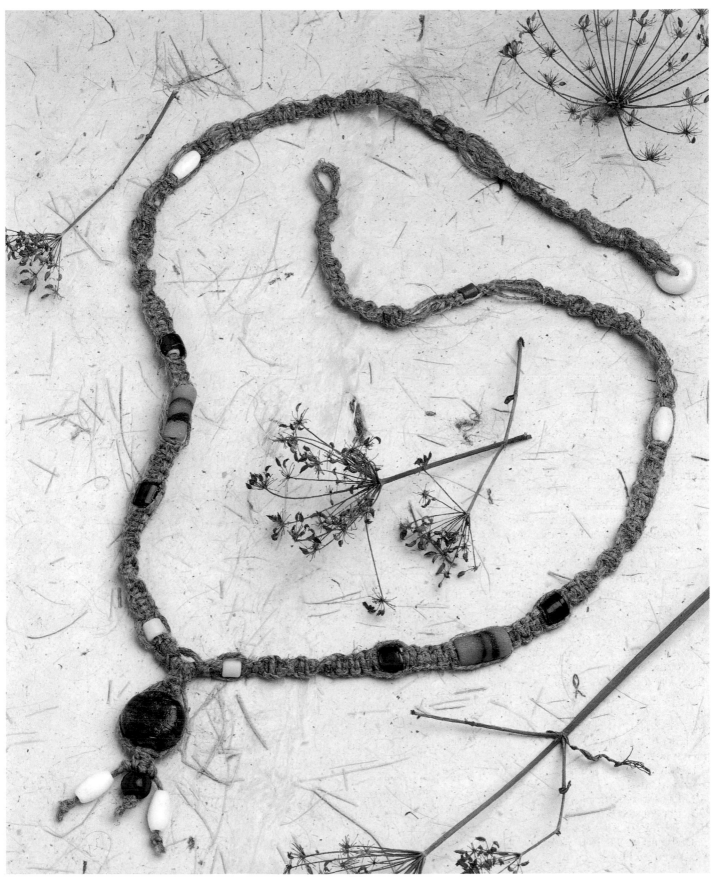

Gala Rhythm

Finished length: 19" (end to end)

MATERIALS
2-1/2 yds. 1mm natural color hemp
    cord
Color striped cylindrical ceramic
    beads—one 1", four 1/2"

KNOTS USED
Overhand Knot
Double Half Hitch
Square Knot

CUTTING CORDS
Cut three 30" cords.

INSTRUCTIONS
1. Fold the 3 cords in half to find and align
    centers.
2. Tie all cords together with an Overhand
    Knot, leaving a 3/4" loop. There are 6
    working cords.
3. Tie rows of Double Half Hitches, alter-
    nating diagonally down to the left and
    diagonally down to the right for 7".
4. Tie a Square Knot using 2 filler cords
    and 4 knotting cords.
5. Thread the 2 filler cords through a 1/2"
    bead.
6. Tie a Square Knot using 2 filler cords
    and 4 knotting cords.
7. Thread the 2 filler cords through a 1/2"
    bead.
8. Tie a Square Knot using 2 filler cords
    and 4 knotting cords.
9. Thread the 2 filler cords through the 1"
    bead.
10. Tie a Square Knot using 2 filler cords
    and 4 knotting cords.
11. Thread the 2 filler cords through a 1/2"
    bead.
12. Tie a Square Knot using 2 filler cords
    and 4 knotting cords.
13. Thread the 2 filler cords through a 1/2"
    bead.
14. Repeat step 3.
15. Tie an Overhand Knot with all cords.
16. Drop down 1/2" and tie 2 Overhand
    Knots on top of each other to create but-
    ton to go through loop. Clip cords.   ◫

Designed by Miche Baskett

Woven Two-Tone Chokers

EMBEDDED BEADS

Pictured right on page 83
Finished length: 13 1/2" (end to end) + braided tie

MATERIALS
4-1/4 yds. 1mm orange hemp cord
3-1/3 yds. 1mm natural color hemp
   cord
Five amber pony beads
Thick white glue

KNOTS USED
Overhand Knot
Half Hitch
Weaving With Cords Together Over
   Stationary Cords
Three-Part Flat Braid

CUTTING CORDS
Cut one 30" orange cord
Cut one 3-1/3-yd. orange cord
Cut two 30" natural cords
Cut two 2-1/2-yd. natural cords

INSTRUCTIONS
1. Place all cords together, aligning one end of them. Fold aligned ends over 1-1/2".
2. Tie an Overhand Knot with all cords, leaving a 3/4" loop. There are 6 working cords.
3. Arrange the 3 short cords with the orange cord in the middle and anchor them with T-pins..
4. Following Fig. 1, weave the 3 long cords together as one back and forth through the 3 anchored cords for 4-1/4".
5. Thread a bead onto the middle (orange) stationary cord.
6. Weave for 3 rows.
7. Repeat steps 5 and 6 three times.
8. Repeat step 5.
9. Weave for 3".
10. Tie a 1-1/4" Half Hitch sinnet around all other cords with the long orange cord.
11. Divide cords into 3 groups of 2 cords each. Braid groups for 5" with a Three-Part Flat Braid.
12. Tie an Overhand Knot with all cords at end of braid. Put glue on knot. When dry, clip cords close to knot. Tie braid through loop at other end of necklace to fasten. ◇

Designed by Miche Baskett

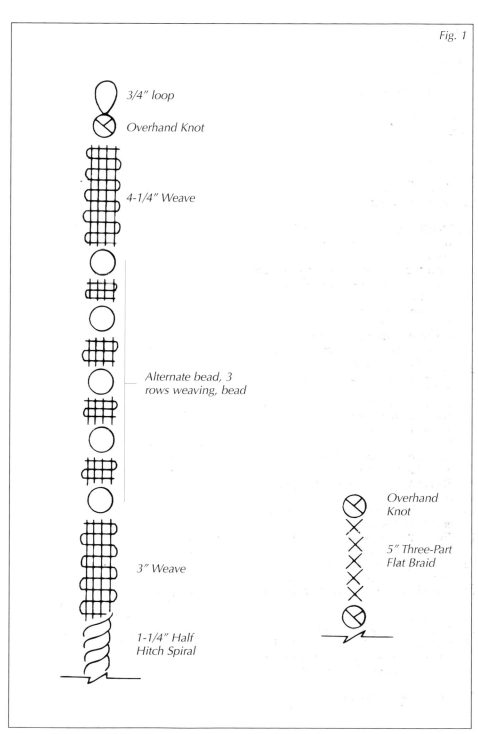

Fig. 1

3/4" loop

Overhand Knot

4-1/4" Weave

Alternate bead, 3
rows weaving, bead

3" Weave

1-1/4" Half
Hitch Spiral

Overhand
Knot

5" Three-Part
Flat Braid

Woven Two-Tone Chokers

WOVEN DRAMA

Pictured left on page 83
Finished length: 16-1/2" (end to end) + braided tie

MATERIALS
4-1/3 yds, 1mm orange hemp cord
3-1/3 yds. 1mm natural-color hemp cord
Three flattened round black beads, 5/8"
  wide
Two round gold beads, 1/2" diam.
Thick white glue

KNOTS USED
Overhand Knot
Half Hitch
Weaving With Cords Successively Over
  Stationary Cords
3-Part Flat Braid

CUTTING CORDS
Cut one 30" orange cord
Cut one 3-1/3-yd. orange cord
Cut two 30" natural cords
Cut two 2-1/2-yd. natural cords

INSTRUCTIONS
1. Place all cords together, aligning one
   end of them. Fold aligned ends over 1-
   1/2".
2. Follow Fig. 1. Tie an Overhand Knot
   with all cords, leaving a 3/4" loop.
3. With the long orange cord, tie a Half
   Hitch sinnet around all other cords
   (covering short ends of cords) for 1-1/4".
   There are 6 working cords: a long and a
   short orange cord and 2 long and 2
   short natural cords.
4. Arrange the 3 short cords with the
   orange cord in the middle and anchor
   them with T-pins..
5. Weave the 3 long cords one at a time
   back and forth across the 3 anchored
   cords (one at a time across from left to
   right, then one at a time across from
   right to left).
6. Thread a black bead onto the middle
   (orange) stationary cord.
7. Weave for 3 rows.
8. Repeat steps 6 and 7 three times, alternating gold and black beads.
9. Repeat step 6.
10. Weave for 3".
11. Tie a 1-1/4" Half Hitch sinnet around all
    other cords with the long orange cord.

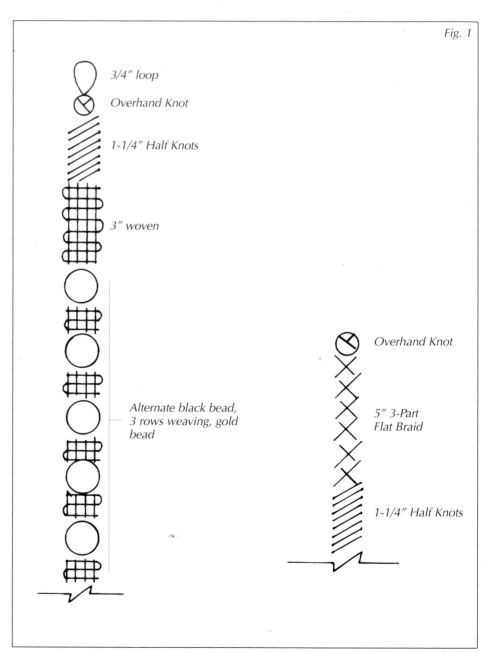

Fig. 1

3/4" loop

Overhand Knot

1-1/4" Half Knots

3" woven

Alternate black bead,
3 rows weaving, gold
bead

Overhand Knot

5" 3-Part
Flat Braid

1-1/4" Half Knots

12. Divide cords into 3 groups of 2 cords
    each. Braid groups for 5" with a Three-
    Part Flat Braid.
13. Tie an Overhand Knot with all cords at
    end of braid. Put glue on knot. When

dry, clip cords close to knot. Tie braid
through loop at other end of necklace to
fasten. ⊠

Designed by Miche Baskett

Knots and Coils

Finished length: 13" (from center back to center front)

MATERIALS
12 yds. 1mm black hemp cord
Three copper coil beads, 5/8" long
Thick white glue

KNOTS USED
Square Knot
Alternating Half Hitches
Overhand Knot

CUTTING CORDS
Cut six 2-yd. cords.

INSTRUCTIONS
1. Center one bead on all 6 cords. Tie 3 Square Knots on each side of bead (using 4 filler cords).

Steps 2-8 are given for one side of necklace. Repeat each step on other side. Follow Fig. 1.

2. Slide another bead on all 6 cords.
3. Tie 6 Square Knots.
4. Divide cords into 3 groups of 2 cords each and tie 60 Alternating Half Hitches with each group. (Some groups may have as few as 58, another as many as 62 as tension may vary; mainly keep them equal lengths.)
5. Tie 6 Square Knots.
6. Divide into 3 groups of 2 cords each and tie 30 Alternating Half Hitches with each group. (Keep groups the same length.)
7. Tie 6 Square Knots.
8. Cut the shortest cord and tie 3 Square Knots. Repeat twice.
9. To join ends, use 2 cords from each end of necklace and tie a Square Knot that is sideways to previous Square Knots (see Fig. 2). Repeat on opposite side. Use the 4 nearest cords to end of necklace and tie a Square Knot around necklace. Cut the 2 shortest cords and tie an Overhand Knot over the Square Knot. Secure knot with thick white glue and clip cord ends close. Repeat on other side of necklace joint. This is a permanent closure. Slip necklace over head to wear. ◇

Designed by Kathryn Gould

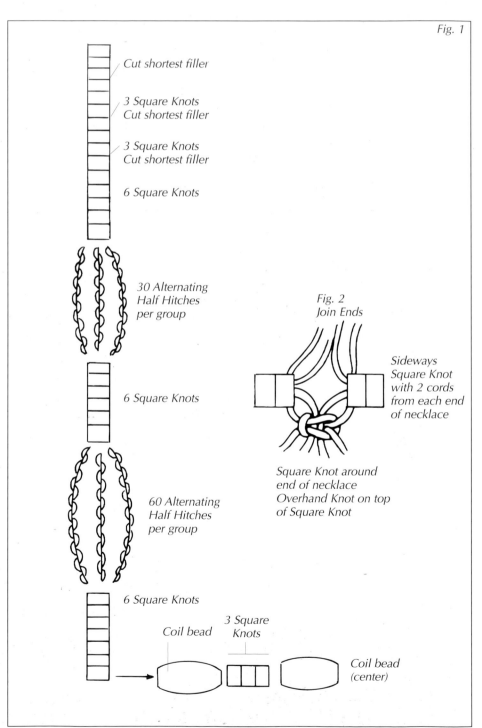

Fig. 1

Cut shortest filler

3 Square Knots
Cut shortest filler

3 Square Knots
Cut shortest filler

6 Square Knots

30 Alternating
Half Hitches
per group

6 Square Knots

60 Alternating
Half Hitches
per group

6 Square Knots

Coil bead

3 Square
Knots

Coil bead
(center)

Fig. 2
Join Ends

Sideways
Square Knot
with 2 cords
from each end
of necklace

Square Knot around
end of necklace
Overhand Knot on top
of Square Knot

Sunshine and Pottery

Finished length: 10-1/4" (from ends to end of pendant bead)

MATERIALS

9 yds. 1mm yellow hemp cord
Brown pottery beads: one 1-1/2" long
    irregular diamond shape; two 3/4"
    round; two 1/4" disk shape
Thick white glue

KNOTS USED

Half Knot
Overhand Knot

CUTTING CORDS

Cut a 6-yd. cord.
Cut three 1-yd. cords.

INSTRUCTIONS

1. Fold the 6-yd. cord in half. The fold
    will form end loop of necklace and
    the 2 cord ends will be knotting
    cords. Fold the three 1-yd. cords in
    half and place fold 1" down from
    fold of 6-yd. cords. These will pro-
    vide 6 filler cords.
2. Tie 5" of Half Knots.
3. Place a round bead on 2 filler cords.
    Bring other fillers and knotting cords
    around bead.
4. Tie 3" of Half Knots.
5. String a small bead onto one of the
    filler cords. String the 1-1/2" bead
    onto the outside knotting cord.
    String the second small bead onto
    same knotting cord. Take cord
    around the small bead and back up
    through large bead. This is center of
    necklace.
6. Work other side of necklace, repeat-
    ing steps 2-4 in reverse.
7. Tie 2 Overhand Knots with all
    cords, one on top of the other. Put
    glue on last knot and clip excess
    cordage. ◇

Designed by Sandy Dye

The Better to See With

COLORFUL SIGHT

Pictured top on page 89
Finished length: 25" (end to end) + earpiece holders

MATERIALS
4 yds. 1mm black hemp cord
3 yds. 1mm turquoise hemp cord
1 yd. each color 1mm yellow, natural,
  and red hemp cord
Two elastic (or stretchable plastic) earpiece holders
Thick white glue

KNOTS USED
Lark's Head
Four-Part Round Braid
Square Knot
Overhand Knot
Wrap Knot

CUTTING CORDS
Cut one 3-yd. black cord.
Cut one 3-yd. turquoise cord.
Cut yellow, natural, red, and black
  wrap cords as needed.

INSTRUCTIONS
1. Fold the 3-yd. cords in half and
   mount to base loop of one earpiece
   holder with a Lark's Head. This creates 4 working cords—2 black and
   2 turquoise.
2. Follow Fig. 1. Braid the 4 cords for
   25" with a Four-Part Round Braid.
3. Thread cords through base loop of
   other earpiece holder. Tie a Square
   Knot, then an Overhand Knot
   around end of braid. Put glue on
   Overhand Knot and clip excess
   cordage.
4. Using black, yellow, red, and natural cords, tie 1/2" long Wrap Knots
   around braid along its length, leaving 2" of space between them. ◇

By Marion Brizendine

Additional project instructions on page 92

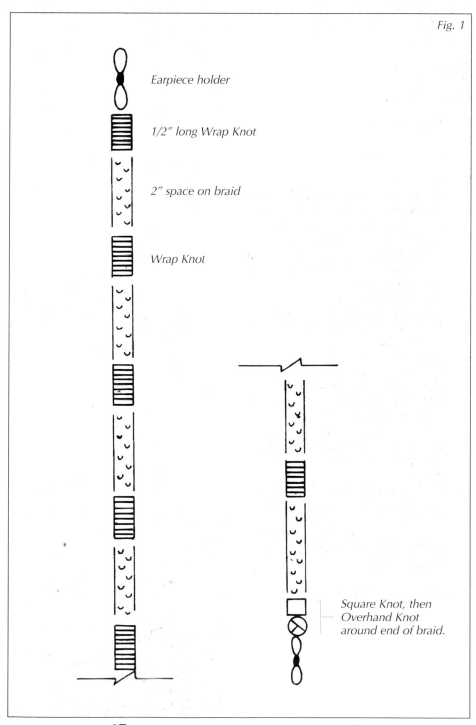

Fig. 1

Earpiece holder

1/2" long Wrap Knot

2" space on braid

Wrap Knot

Square Knot, then
Overhand Knot
around end of braid.

The Better to See With

THE EYES HAVE IT

Pictured bottom on page 89
Finished length: 23" (end to end) + earpiece holders

MATERIALS
7 yds. 1mm natural color hemp cord
Two medium blue oval wood beads,
   1/2" long
Two dark blue round beads, 1/4" diam.
Two crimp pieces for ends, 1/2" long
Two elastic (or stretchable plastic) ear-
   piece holders

KNOTS USED
Three-Part Flat Braid
Half Knot
Square Knot

CUTTING
Cut two 5-1/3 yd. cords
Cut one 1-2/3 yd. cords

INSTRUCTIONS
1. Align ends of the 3 cords. Braid for 4" with a Three-Part Flat Braid.
2. Fold 1/2" of braid through bottom of elastic loop piece back over braided section. Secure with a crimp piece around both layers of braid as close to elastic loop piece as possible. Clip any excess cord at bottom of crimp piece.
3. Follow Fig. 1. Where braided section ended, thread all 3 cord ends through oval bead. Place long cords on outsides for knotting cords and short cord in center for filler cord.
4. Tie a 3-1/2" sinnet of Half Knots
5. Thread a round bead on filler cord.
6. Tie a 9-1/4" sinnet of Square Knots.
7. Repeat step 5.
8. Repeat step 4.
9. Thread all 3 cords through an oval bead.
10. Braid for 4" with a Three-Part Flat Braid.
11. Repeat step 2. ◇

Designed by Miche Baskett

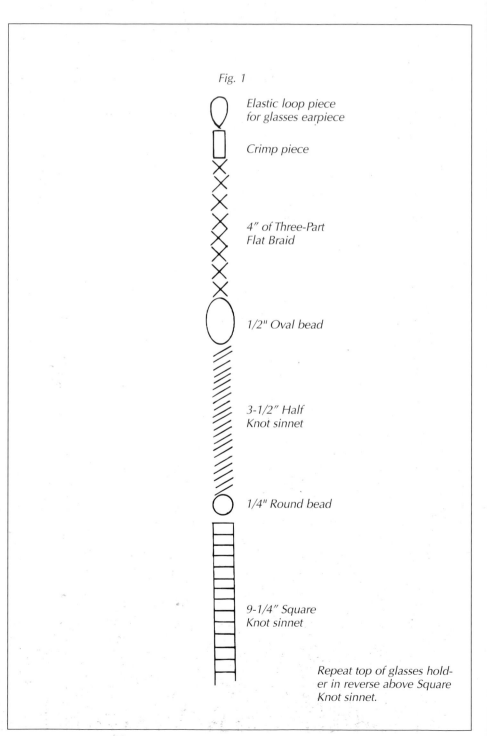

Fig. 1

Elastic loop piece
for glasses earpiece

Crimp piece

4" of Three-Part
Flat Braid

1/2" Oval bead

3-1/2" Half
Knot sinnet

1/4" Round bead

9-1/4" Square
Knot sinnet

*Repeat top of glasses hold-
er in reverse above Square
Knot sinnet.*

On-the-Go Keyrings

BRIGHT TOUCH

Pictured right on page 91
Finished length: 5″ + ring

MATERIALS
4 yds. 1mm natural-color hemp cord
Keyring, 1-1/4″ diam.
3 red wood oval beads, 3/8″ long

KNOTS USED
Lark's Head
Square Knot
Overhand Knot

CUTTING CORDS
Cut four 1-yd. cords

INSTRUCTIONS
1. Follow Fig 1. Fold the 4 cords in half and mount side by side on keyring with Lark's Heads. There will be 8 working cords. Number them 1-8, left to right.
2. Tie a Square Knot with cords 3-6. Move cords 3 and 6 up out of the way. Tie a Square Knot with cords 2, 4, 5, and 7.
3. Move cords 2 and 7 up out of the way. Tie a Square Knot with cords 1, 4, 5, and 8.
4. Thread cords 4-5 (center 2 cords) through a bead.
5. Renumber cords from left to right.
6. Tie a Square Knot with cords 1, 4, 5, and 8.
7. Move cords 1 and 8 up out of the way. Tie a Square Knot with cords 2, 4, 5, and 7.
8. Move cords 2 and 7 up out of the way. Tie a Square Knot with cords 3-6.
9. Repeat steps 4-8 twice.
10. Bring all cords together and tie an Overhand Knot. Cut cords off evenly 1-1/4″ beyond Overhand Knot. ◌

Designed by Miche Baskett

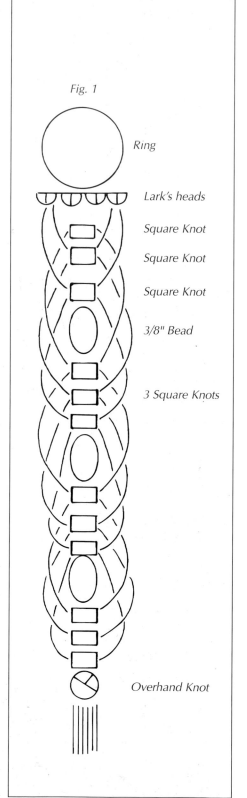

Fig. 1

Ring

Lark's heads

Square Knot

Square Knot

Square Knot

3/8″ Bead

3 Square Knots

Overhand Knot

CARNIVAL RIDE

Pictured left on page 91
Finished length: 5″ + ring

MATERIALS
1-1/2 yds. each color of 1mm hemp cord in 6 colors
Keyring, 1-1/4″ diam.
Concho with prongs
Thick white glue

KNOTS USED
Lark's Head
Alternating Square Knots
Double Half Hitch
Overhand Knot

CUTTING CORDS
Cut a 1-yd. cord of 6 different colors (6 cords)
Cut a 1/2-yd. cord of 6 different colors (6 cords)

INSTRUCTIONS
1. Mount each 1-yd. cord to keyring with Lark's Heads. This creates 12 working cords.
2. Tie 8 rows of Alternating Square Knots, starting with a 3-knot row and ending with a 2-knot row. Then tie a Square Knot with the center 4 cords.
3. Using outside cords on each side as holding cords, Double Half Hitch other cords diagonally down to center. Do not Double Half Hitch holding cords together. Repeat for a second row.
4. Tie the 4 holding cords (one from each row from each side) in an Overhand Knot below last Double Half Hitch row at center. Put glue on back of last Double Half Hitch row and cut cords to 1/8″ long.
5. Place all 1/2-yd. cords together. Attach the bunch above Overhand Knot between Double Half Hitch rows with one giant Lark's Head.
6. Attach concho with prongs to Alternating Square Knot section where desired. ◌

By Marion Brizendine

A Study In Blue

TOUCHES OF BLUE CHOKER

Pictured right on page 93

Finished length: 14-1/2" (end to end). To lengthen, add more Square Knots after last tube bead on each side.

MATERIALS

6-2/3 yd. 1mm natural-color hemp
  cord
24" 1mm purple hemp cord
Five cobalt blue glass pony beads
Six silver tube beads, 1/2" long
One silver cylinder bead, 1-1/2" long
Thick white glue

KNOTS USED

Square Knot
Wrap Knot

CUTTING CORDS

Cut four 1-1/2-yd. natural cords.
Cut one 24" natural cord.
Cut two 12" purple cords

INSTRUCTIONS

1. Follow Fig. 1. String a pony bead to the center of the four 1-1/2-yd. cords. Tie 2 Square Knots on each side of bead.
Work steps 2-11 first on one side of necklace, then on other side, working from center toward ends.
2. Add a tube bead with hole perpendicular to necklace by threading one knotting cord through bead in one direction and the other knotting cord through same bead in the opposite direction. Let filler cords simply cross over bead. Bring all cords together again on other side of bead.
3. Tie 2 Square Knots
4. String a pony bead on all 4 cords.
5. Tie 6 Square Knots.
6. Thread the 2 filler cords through a tube bead. (This one is not perpendicular to necklace.)
7. Tie 5 Square Knots
8. Repeat step 4.
9. Repeat step 7.
10. Repeat step 6.
11. Tie 9 Square Knots.
12. Loop end: With a separate 24" natural cord, tie a 2-1/2" long Wrap Knot around the 4 cords. Fold wrapped section back to end of necklace to form a loop. Tie 2 Square Knots around end of

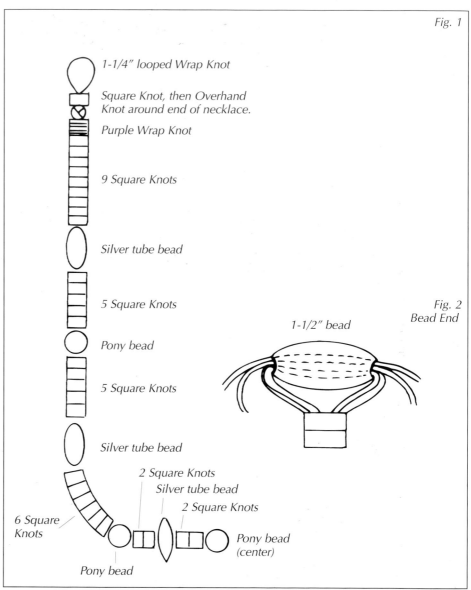

Fig. 1

1-1/4" looped Wrap Knot

Square Knot, then Overhand Knot around end of necklace.

Purple Wrap Knot

9 Square Knots

Silver tube bead

5 Square Knots

Pony bead

5 Square Knots

Silver tube bead

6 Square Knots

Pony bead

2 Square Knots
Silver tube bead
2 Square Knots

Pony bead (center)

Fig. 2
Bead End

1-1/2" bead

necklace. Glue last knot and clip excess cordage.

13. Bead end (Fig. 2): Thread 2 cords through the 1-1/2" bead in one direction and the other 2 cords through same bead in the opposite direction. Bring cords back to end of necklace. Tie 2 Square Knots around end of

necklace. Glue last knot and clip excess cordage.

14. With a 12" purple cord, tie a Wrap Knot around end of necklace (up to loop or bead); repeat on other end. Clip excess cordage. ◇

Designed by Marion Brizendine

92

A Study In Blue

NATURAL BEAUTY NECKLACE

Pictured left on page 93
Finished length: 17" (end to end)

MATERIALS
5 yds. + 45" 1mm cobalt blue hemp
Natural wood beads—six 3/8" round,
  one 1" oval
Natural wood shank button, 5/8" wide
Thick white glue

KNOTS USED
Overhand Knot
Half Knot
Square Knot (no fillers)

CUTTING
Cut one 5-yd. cord
Cut one 45" cord

INSTRUCTIONS
1. Fold cords in half to find centers. Tie cords together with an Overhand Knot, leaving a 1/2" loop. Follow Fig. 1 as you work.
2. Tie 3-1/2" of Half Knots.
3. Add a round bead to center cords.
4. Tie 1" of Half Knots.
5. Add a round bead to center cords.
6. Tie 1" of Half Knots.
7. Add a round bead to center cords.
8. Tie 1" of Half Knots.
9. Add an oval bead to center cords.
10. Tie 1" of Half Knots.
11. Add a round bead to center cords.
12. Tie 1" of Half Knots.
13. Add a round bead to center cords.
14. Tie 1" of Half Knots.
15. Add a round bead to center cords.
16. Tie 3-1/2" of Half Knots.
17. Tie a natural wooden shank button on center cords. Tie all cords together with a Square Knot (use 4 knotting cords, no fillers). Apply a dot of thick white glue to ending knot. Clip ends. ◇

Designed by Patti Cox

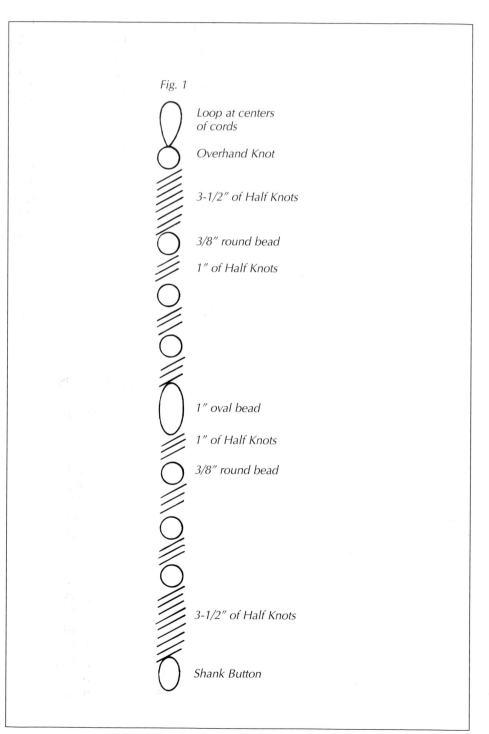

Fig. 1

Loop at centers of cords

Overhand Knot

3-1/2" of Half Knots

3/8" round bead

1" of Half Knots

1" oval bead

1" of Half Knots

3/8" round bead

3-1/2" of Half Knots

Shank Button

Metric Conversions

INCHES TO MILLIMETERS AND CENTIMETERS

Inches	MM	CM
1/8	3	.3
1/4	6	.6
3/8	10	1.0
1/2	13	1.3
5/8	16	1.6
3/4	19	1.9
7/8	22	2.2
1	25	2.5
1-1/4	32	3.2
1-1/2	38	3.8
1-3/4	44	4.4
2	51	5.1
3	76	7.6
4	102	10.2
5	127	12.7
6	152	15.2
7	178	17.8
8	203	20.3
9	229	22.9
10	254	25.4
11	279	27.9
12	305	30.5

YARDS TO METERS

Yards	Meters
1/8	.11
1/4	.23
3/8	.34
1/2	.46
5/8	.57
3/4	.69
7/8	.80
1	.91
2	1.83
3	2.74
4	3.66
5	4.57
6	5.49
7	6.40
8	7.32
9	8.23
10	9.14

Index